ADULT EDUCATION IN AMERICA

A POLICY ASSESSMENT OF ADULT LEARNING

BEN WOOD JOHNSON

TESKO

TESKO PUBLISHING PRESS
Middletown, Pennsylvania

Printed in the United States of America/Library of Congress

Johnson, Ben W., 1975-
Adult Education in America: A Policy Assessment of Adult Learning / Ben Wood Johnson. —Tesko Publishing ed.

Includes bibliographical references and index.
ISBN-13: 978-1-948600-11-8 (pbk.)
ISBN-10: 1-948600-11-0

2024 Edition. This book was first published in 2019/Copyright © 2024 by Ben Wood Johnson

The information illustrated in this book was compiled for a school project. The analysis is based on class notes and other materials.

1. Education, adult—United States. 2. Policy assessment. 3. Adult learning. 4. Higher education. I. Johnson, Ben Wood.

Johnson, Ben Wood
Adult Education in America: A Policy Assessment of Adult Learning

Publishing House Info:

For information

Eduka Solutions Press
A BWEC, LLC Company
330 W. Main St. #214
Middletown, PA 17057
United States of America
www.benwoodedconsulting.com

Tesko Publishing Press
A BWEC, LLC Company
P.O. Box 214
Middletown, PA 17057
United States of America
www.teskopublishing.com

Ben Wood & Sons Press
A BWEC, LLC Company
New York and New Jersey
United States of America
www.bwsp.com

Ben Wood J. Books
A BWEC, LLC Company
Middletown, PA 17057
United States of America
www.benwoodjbooks.com

This book is printed on acid-free paper.

06 07 08 09 10 11 12 10 9 8 7 6 5 4 3 2 1

Acquisition Editor:	Woody Olive
Production Editor:	Gerard Pierre
Associate Editor:	Dann Vitale
Copy Editor 1:	Viau Polo
Copy Editor 2:	Den Vitale
Proofreader:	Benny Johnson
Cover Designer:	Wood Vitale and Viau Polo

TESKO PUBLISHING
An independent publishing house

Tesko Publishing/My Eduka Solutions

Middletown, Pennsylvania

Tesko Publishing

Ben Wood Educational Consulting, LLC

BWEC, LLC

BEN WOOD POST

www.benwoodpost.org

Adult Education in America

A Policy Assessment of Adult Learning

BEN WOOD JOHNSON

To Yves Charles

CONTENTS

ACKNOWLEDGMENTS

During the intellectually demanding process of writing this book, various individuals played pivotal roles, which deserve explicit public recognition. Chief among them is Dr. Roger Shouse, whose invaluable feedback enriched not just the segments but the entire scope of this manuscript. His keen insights and discerning commentary significantly increased the scholarly quality of the work. Every page marked with annotations reflected his wisdom. They provided a powerful mix of motivation. They also offered helpful criticism.

Equally worthy of my gratitude is Mynn Olive, whose dedication to the project materialized in a meticulous review of the manuscript. The diligence shown in this act contributed significantly to the intellectual rigor of the book. Olive's thorough evaluation was a key aspect of refining the work to its ultimate and polished state. It ensured that it met the highest standards of academic excellence.

I express my deep gratitude to my editor, Chan Olive. His diligence and discerning insights have helped shape this book. His unwavering commitment and extraordinary patience throughout this project have been remarkable.

Thank you to the Tesko Publishing Press team. Your professional support and commitment throughout the project were crucial to the completion of the book. You played an important role in transforming this literary vision into a tangible reality. I thank Wol Denny for investing valuable time in reviewing the manuscript. I acknowledge Wood Vitale for his ability to format the manuscript.

I am grateful to Gerard Pierre for his role in orchestrating this project. The feedback that Dann Vitale provided was incredibly valuable and has been appreciated. He proofread multiple manuscripts, for which I am infinitely grateful. Wood Vitale and Viau Polo deserve special recognition for creating a visually compelling cover design. These contributors made this book possible.

This revised edition had also been edited and revamped by Runedan and Zean Production. The collective input of these remarkable individuals transformed what was once a burgeoning concept into a comprehensive scholarly work. The expertise they offered significantly increased the intellectual quality of the manuscript. It imbued the book with depth and richness that would have been unreachable in isolation.

My heartfelt thanks to everyone involved in this journey. Your contributions have enriched the realization of this academic endeavor. You are the foundation for its success. I extend my deepest appreciation to you all for your wonderful support.

Thank you.

—Dr. Jay

Keywords: education, adult education, higher education, and school policy

PREFACE

Although education can be a curse, knowledge is always a blessing. —BWJ, 2017

In the fall of 2009, I was immersed in the academic landscape of Pennsylvania State University (commonly referred to as Penn State). As a student majoring in Educational Leadership and School Administration, I had the challenging, yet invigorating task of compiling a research paper on adult education for my final project. The undertaking was nothing short of trivial; it required rigorous intellectual labor and empirical analysis.

On completion of the project, the paper received immediate acclaim. Classmates from various intellectual backgrounds provided their feedback. Some individuals expressed their agreement with the findings. They echoed my sentiments about the state of adult education in the United States. An intriguing dialogue emerged that sparked collective reflections on the successes and failures of our educational system.

The acknowledgment extended beyond the student body. Dr. Roger Shouse, the course instructor, conveyed his admiration by awarding the paper a high grade. His comments in the margins served as both an affirmation and a constructive criticism. He praised the thoroughness of my research, as well as the depth of analysis shown in the document.

Encouraged by Dr. Shouse, I felt compelled to dig into the topic further. He provided detailed guidelines to enhance my investigative skills. This laid the foundational path for future explorations on the subject. The experience was intellectually enriching. It improved my academic journey and reinforced my intellectual identity.

My educational odyssey in America was not without its trials. Challenges arose that tested my resilience. These challenges had a profound impact on my well-being. These hardships, while formidable, contributed to my growth and offered invaluable life lessons.

When a close friend recently revealed his aspirations to return to academia and pursue a graduate degree, he sought advice from my reservoir of experience. Given that I navigated academia both as an adult learner and as a foreign student, I could offer unique insights. I immediately warned him about the imminent obstacles. I stress the necessity of resilience and persistence.

This reflection on my college days evoked a desire to contribute more substantially to the discourse on adult education. I considered writing a book that would summarize and build on my previous research. It became important for me to review the paper I initially submitted for Dr. Shouse's class. I revised the document and transformed it into a more thorough analysis on the subject.

The present edition should function as a dual purpose. It is both a storyline and a scholarly examination of adult education in the United States. That way, I was able to turn the initial assignment into a more enhanced compilation of thoughts, which offers the reader a greater understanding of the concept of adult learning in that part of the world.

Although my journey as an adult learner through American academia was punctuated with moments of triumph, it also bears the weight of failure. Several of the obstacles I faced were explicitly academic. They were born from intellectual challenges that I was unable to overcome. Others, on the other hand, were rooted in personal difficulties, as I found myself entangled in situations that seemed impossible to navigate successfully.

Left to my own devices, I often felt isolated in the labyrinthine structure of higher education. The lack of institutional support exacerbated the difficulties that I faced. In fact, sometimes school officials not only did not help but also created the very barriers that impeded my progress. Navigating through an educational environment as a foreigner presented a unique set of challenges. This experience amplified my sense of alienation.

Although this book offers a concise exploration, it does not encompass the full spectrum of my challenges within the American educational system. Instead, it focuses on the struggles adults face commonly in similar settings.

Subsequent chapters will dive into specific scenarios that have had lasting impacts on those who attempt to carve out an academic path later in life.

The quest for a college degree is not an isolated endeavor; it is a pursuit that many adults, like my friend and perhaps even you at the moment, are actively engaged in. The insights gleaned from my own experiences might be influential in improving your academic journey. This work aims to serve as a substantive addition to academic discourse and, if possible, to your personal library. Let us dive into the complexities and nuances of the educational experience for adult learners in the United States.

Good reading!
Ben Wood Johnson, Ph.D.

Updated
January 2024

INTRODUCTION

INTRODUCING ADULT LEARNING

In the United States, the quest for education can be a daunting experience. For whatever reason, some individuals have no choice but to head back to school. While some head to school by choice, others do so out of necessity. For some, life circumstances forced them to head back to school.

In many cases, going to school, whether for the first time or in the hope of acquiring new skills, can be a tragic ordeal. Individuals who used to be someone back home may feel the need to go to school to build their new life in America. Regardless, when older individuals choose the path of an educational institution to enrich their mind, they become adult learners.

The road to adult learning is not paved in gold. The path to an education, at least for most adult learners, is fraught with an intricate array of challenges. Some difficulties tend to originate directly from academic rigor, while others originate in pedagogical systems, which cannot adapt to adult learning styles or their life circumstances. A nonnegligible set of impediments is generally social. In similar instances, discrimination often becomes a formidable obstacle, which most adult learners must face. But this discrimination often presents itself in a variety of ways. It generally impacts educational experiences in a variety of settings.

This edition does not delve into the issue of discrimination in schools. However, it is important to glance at these issues as we move along in our analysis. Nonetheless, the book centers on the reality of adult learning and the plight of adult learners in the United States.

Within the hallowed halls of higher education, adult learners face policies that, although benign, harbor inherent inequities. Although these treatments may not overtly display prejudice, they often have a detrimental impact on the adult learner. This impact can be palpable. It often leaves an indelible mark on the learner's educational trajectories. Therefore, it is essential to scrutinize these opaque practices, which perpetuate systemic inequality in adult education in the United States.

Adult learners face a multitude of challenges in their educational journey. They deal with problems in distance education online. Enduring emotional trials is something they do. They suffer from a lack of motivation. They face hurdles when trying to go back to college. Recognizing and addressing these challenges is essential to create effective and inclusive educational environments for adult learners.

Subtle, yet pernicious, forms of dishonesty often characterize the treatment of adult learners, particularly in higher educational institutions. Both older and younger college students endure experiences that, while socially unacceptable if exposed, frequently go unchallenged. These practices persist, veiled behind the mask of social norms, or misguided educational policies, further complicating the journey of adult learners.

This edition is a meticulous examination of the prevailing treatment offered to adult learners within higher education institutions. It delves into the consequential policy implications related to adult education and offers a dissection of the many obstacles that these learners face in their pursuit of scholarly enlightenment. Through a nuanced approach, the book aims to address several vital questions.

Although this work does not cover the entire spectrum of adult education, it delves into selected aspects that merit scholarly attention. A critical area of focus is the pedagogical implications that specifically pertain to adult learning. The aim is to illuminate the nuanced obstacles that often thwart adults in realizing their academic aspirations, whether in a college or a university setting.

The book surveys specific challenges that not only obstruct adult learners but also potentially discourage any individual from flourishing in a highly competitive educational environment. This examination aims to shed light on the multifaceted hurdles that adult learners must navigate. The aim of this work, though brief, is to dissect these challenges as thoroughly as possible. Another aim is to provide stakeholders with actionable information. This includes educators and policymakers who are dedicated to improving the educational experiences of adult learners.

Among the critical issues under scrutiny are: 1) the defining criteria for adult learners; 2) the actors involved in the policy-making process for adult education; 3) the pedagogical frameworks that guide adult learning experiences; and 4) the host of cultural, social, and environmental factors that contribute to the unique challenges facing this demographic. This comprehensive analysis aims not only to highlight the complexities, but it also instigates meaningful dialogue and policy reform in adult education.

In the pages of this concise, yet, powerful, volume eight chapters are organized into four distinct thematic streams. They include personal, policy, pedagogical, and social streams. While the book itself is not rooted in empirical analysis, it draws on a diverse array of authoritative sources to fortify its arguments. These sources span academic literature and informal works. They contribute to the rich intellectual fabric of the text.

It is the aspiration of this endeavor to shed light on some of the multifaceted realities inherent in adult education, particularly within the United States. Although the scope of this work is limited, it seeks to engage with various phenomena that encapsulate the experience of adult learning. With a consistent lens focused on the American educational landscape, the aim is to provoke thoughtful examination and incite dialogue about these pressing issues.

The thematic streams highlighted in this context function as a structural foundation for the task at hand. They facilitate a detailed analysis of the varied obstacles and possibilities encountered by adult learners. By navigating these carefully curated sections, the reader will acquire an expansive understanding of adult education that extends beyond simplistic stereotypes or preconceived notions. In so doing, this work seeks to offer a valuable contribution to the academic discourse surrounding adult education. Let us delve into the debate further.

A PERSONAL STREAM

-1-

UNDERSTANDING ADULT LEARNING

The questions surrounding the definition and qualifications for adult learning have perplexed educators and policymakers for a long time. The labyrinth of adult education continues to be a topic that has garnered substantial interest over the past few decades, particularly in the United States (Travers, 2013). However, it should be noted that the federal government of the United States has consistently played a pivotal role in the formation of educational policies tailored to adult learners.

While this scholarly effort refrains from an exhaustive examination of practical issues, it offers critical evaluations of selected challenges that negatively impact adult learners. The focus here lies predominantly in dissecting these complexities from a policy-oriented point of view. It seeks to distill the crucial elements that policymakers must consider when crafting initiatives to enhance adult learning experiences.

Far from an exhilarating journey, the realm of adult education can often seem daunting, even bleak. Navigating such a landscape is not a trivial feat. It requires more than mere will or intent. Educational attainment is a linchpin in the machinery of social mobility, particularly in contemporary social contexts. Despite its centrality, access to education remains markedly limited for a substantial number of individuals.

The stakes in acquiring an education are perceived to be monumental. Loveless (2019) identified the emotionally charged atmosphere that often envelopes adult learners; they frequently express trepidation about reentering an academic setting (Loveless, 2019, 2023). Concerns range from financial implications to time commitments, and even to the potential awkwardness of sharing a classroom with significantly younger individuals (Loveless, 2019, 2023). These issues only represent the surface of a much more complex conundrum facing adult learners throughout their educational journey.

Adult learners face various challenges in education, which can affect their learning outcomes and success. One challenge is the specific difficulties faced by adult learners in distance education online. Research has shown that adult learners may face challenges such as time management, technological problems, lack of social interaction, and self-motivation in online learning environments Kara et al. (2019). These challenges can hinder their participation and progress in their educational pursuits (Kara et al., 2019).

Another challenge that adult learners may also face is math anxiety. Studies have found that adult learners may experience higher levels of math anxiety compared with traditional undergraduate students. Math anxiety has the potential to adversely affect an individual's self-concept and self-efficacy in mathematics. This can cause a decrease in confidence. It can also result in deficient performance in math-related subjects (Jameson & Fusco, 2014). Granted, addressing math anxiety and providing support to adult learners to develop math skills can help mitigate this challenge.

Adult learners in higher education face emotional obstacles. Most adult learners may experience anxiety and self-consciousness about their acceptance, place in a college environment, and the ability to perform as undergraduate students. These emotional challenges can affect their confidence, motivation, and general well-being, potentially hindering their educational progress (Kasworm, 2008). Creating a supportive and inclusive learning environment that addresses the emotional needs of adult learners is crucial in overcoming these challenges.

Motivation is another key factor that influences the participation of adult learners in higher education. Research has shown that adult learners are motivated by a variety of factors, including personal growth, career advancement, and the desire for new knowledge and skills (Sogunro, 2015). Therefore, understanding and addressing the motivating factors of adult learners can help educators design programs and interventions that improve their participation and persistence in their own education.

There are barriers that impact the return of adult learners to college. These barricades can include financial restrictions, family responsibilities, lack of confidence, and limited access to educational resources and support systems. Overcoming these blockades requires targeted interventions and support services that address the specific needs and circumstances of adult learners (Osam et al., 2017).

CHANGING TIMES IN EDUCATION

In the days of a not-so-distant past, educational institutions were viewed as sanctuaries for young people, spaces dedicated to the pursuits of knowledge, personal growth, and youth enjoyment. Rarely did these establishments serve as educational havens for adults who, for a variety of reasons, had missed their earlier opportunity for formal education. The stereotype said that schools were not appropriate venues for those who had already grappled with life's complex challenges.

Nowadays, the common belief is that the educational landscape has drastically improved. School settings are, some observers are convinced, more receptive and much more welcoming to adult learners. Of course, there are differing opinions on the matter.

There is no doubt that the landscape of education has undergone a dramatic transformation. Over the past several decades, a change in basic assumptions has occurred in the perception and availability of adult education, particularly in the United States. Critics and scholars agree with that perspective. The once narrow gates to education have expanded significantly. This has ushered in a more democratized form of learning. It could be said that an education is now accessible to anyone who seeks it.

The discussions surrounding the topic of segregation in educational institutions are now perceived by many as archaic. Current conversations veer toward inclusivity as the defining feature of contemporary education. Some people strongly assert that education should be a universal right. At the very least, they believe that it should be something attainable for everyone. This includes all individuals, regardless of age, race, or social status. This perspective promotes the notion that anyone who desires an education should not be barred from receiving it. Nonetheless, it would be remiss to assert that the educational landscape has reached a utopian state of perfect inclusivity.

Contrary to popular presumptions, numerous instances reveal that access to education is not universally fair. In fact, the inequalities present in the broader social fabric often manifest in educational settings. It is an inescapable reality that societal biases and prejudices permeate educational environments. Therefore, while education has made notable strides toward becoming more inclusive, it simultaneously reflects the complex and sometimes disconcerting social dynamics that exist outside its walls.

The assumption that every student should or could have an identical educational experience is fundamentally flawed. Such a concept neglects the complex realities that form the educational system. It does not account for the various elements that contribute to the diverse experiences of the students. In other words, this monolithic viewpoint does not fit the inherently varied nature of education, where disparities are not only common but often systemic.

To extend this argument, one must recognize that a society is rarely, if ever, a level playing field. Although it is beyond the scope of this discussion to dive into all the nuances of societal inequities, it is crucial to note that these disparities do not affect all individuals in the same way. Various factors contribute to this differential impact. This further complicates the narrative around educational equity.

When one narrows the focus to specific axes of identity, such as race, gender, or ethnicity, the complexities surrounding educational inequities grow exponentially. In fact, these identity markers often serve as barriers that disproportionately affect certain groups. Factors such as racial background, religious affiliation, and socioeconomic status exacerbate these educational challenges. It is vital to recognize that the status of being an adult learner does little to mitigate the educational hurdles one might face, which are already magnified by the aforementioned factors. Therefore, while the educational system has made advances toward inclusion, its complexities and inequalities continue to mirror the intricate societal dynamics that feed into it.

EDUCATION AS RIGHTS

The term "education" often generates diverse interpretations and complex debates. While the full scope of its definition remains beyond the purview of the present analysis, education can be universally understood as the intricate process of transmitting knowledge from one individual to another. Despite the complexity surrounding the concept, there is a wide consensus that education is a fundamental human right.

Within the framework of social development, education serves as a means of understanding the social context in which individuals operate. It functions as an avenue for personal growth. But it also serves as a catalyst for collective advancement. By educating themselves, individuals not only acquire knowledge for their own benefit, but also gain an understanding of the rights they possess, along with the rights that others have, within their social setting.

On the contrary, education remains contentious when viewed as a privilege, accessible only to a select few. This perspective engenders discriminatory practices, often manifested through age-related barriers that hinder adult learners. Age-based discrimination thus emerges as a considerable obstacle for those who diverge from the conventional student archetype.

Many educational institutions allocate little resources and attention to adult learners. This leaves them unsupported in their academic pursuits. The system appears to be predisposed to favor the younger demographic. It often neglects the unique needs and challenges that adult learners often face. Despite overwhelming evidence in the scholarly literature supporting the differentiation between adult and traditional learners, the education system remains unaccommodating to the former.

Although the topic remains too expansive to examine exhaustively here, the barriers facing adult learners are not inconsequential. The education system, although considered by many to be a cornerstone of both personal and collective success, has to date shown a woeful inadequacy in its support of adult learners. Whether rooted in age-based discrimination or systemic design, these challenges underscore the urgent need for comprehensive reform to make education more inclusive and equitable.

Navigating a university campus as an adult presents a series of unique challenges; not least among them is the pervasive sense of awkwardness. Subtle age markers, such as gray hair or facial wrinkles, often become points of contention. They cast adult learners in a light that sharply differs from their younger counterparts. While strides have been made to facilitate a more inclusive academic environment, older learners still face significant hurdles in seamlessly blending with younger students.

In the past, an older adult on a college campus was met with an air of curiosity, if not outright discomfort. Far from being welcomed as equals, these individuals were viewed through the narrow lens of stereotypical assumptions. The divergence in lifestyles between older and traditional students was palpable. From social interactions to academic pursuits, the chasm was frequently insurmountable. This reality often relegated the adult learner to the status of an outlier. They became a metaphorical "alien" among their peers.

For many adults, the prospect of returning to the academic sphere is likened to a penance, an unsettling shift from familiar terrains. The challenges they face frequently extend beyond the walls of the classroom and touch on complex, often deeply personal, topics. The capacity to endure the rigor of academic life, both mentally and financially, remains elusive for a sizable number of people considering this path. Therefore, labeling the experience as merely "difficult" would be a gross understatement; it is an undertaking fraught with complexities that defy easy categorization.

Reentering the academic realm as an adult involves a high-stake balancing act, one that demands not just academic acumen but also emotional resilience and logistical agility. This complexity is a testament to the systemic inadequacies that continue to plague adult education. It is a sobering reality. This underscores the urgent need for educational reforms. These reforms should recognize the unique challenges of adult learners. They should also acknowledge the contributions of adult learners.

The journey of higher education as an adult learner requires keen awareness and tact. Each step taken on campus serves as a tighter walk. Balance academic pursuits with a set of unspoken but palpable societal expectations. Exercising discretion becomes not just advisable but imperative.

It is true that in years past, the environment of academia was much less inviting for mature learners. Negative perceptions were widespread. This discernment pushed adult students to the fringes of educational communities. Indeed, unless you occupied a role of institutional authority, such as administrator or professor, your presence on campus would be met with skepticism, even disdain. The predominant sentiment was that older people should not share educational spaces with their younger traditional counterparts.

This exclusionary posture found concrete expression in institutional policies. Elementary and secondary educational institutions, for example, offered courses specifically designed for adult learners but confined them to less desirable time slots, typically in the evening or late at night. This separation perpetuated the misconception that adult education was an afterthought, a less significant annex for the broader academic enterprise.

A PUSH FOR INTEGRATION

Navigating the academic landscape as an adult learner has recently become a subject of increased discourse, with growing efforts to amalgamate these mature students into traditional settings. However, for many, the experience remains fraught with tension and unease. While the age disparities between older and younger students represent one layer of complexity, a broader spectrum of issues begs consideration in this academic debate.

The social dynamics on a college campus can escalate the challenges for adult learners, particularly those who are older than their peers. Perception of age can elicit unwarranted assumptions: Students may misidentify older learners as faculty or even parents. For men, social scrutiny can manifest itself in even more insidious forms. It can lead to baseless criminal suspicion. Campus security officers may subject these older male students to unwarranted checks, propelled by unjustified, albeit potent, stereotypes.

Progress in educational inclusion cannot be overlooked. Historic segregationist policies, exemplified by doctrines such as "separate but equal," have thankfully been removed both in practice and in law from the American educational framework. Despite these strides, an equitable academic experience remains elusive for many. Students of color, as often evidenced in public discourse, still face obstacles to educational achievement. This suggests that the path towards a fully inclusive educational environment is far from being realized.

The landmark ruling of Plessy v. Ferguson in 1896 (Cornell Law, 2010b; *Plessy v. Ferguson*, 1896) initially upheld the constitutionality of racially segregated facilities (History.com Editors, 2009; Linder, 2019; National Museum of American History, Behring Center, n.d.; *Separate but Equal: Segregation in the Public Schools*, n.d.). It was only through subsequent legal battles—Brown v. Board of Education of Topeka (1954) (*Brown v. Board of Education*, 1954; Cornell Law, 2010a), Brown v. Board of Education (Brown II) (1955) (Brown, 1955; *Brown v. Board of Education*, 1955), and Griffin

v. School Board of Prince Co. (1964) (*Griffin v. School Bd. Of Prince Edward Cty.*, 1964)—that the judiciary cemented the notion that "racially segregated schools are inherently unequal" (Linder, 2019).

Although the educational/legal landscape has undergone significant transformation, the presumption that American educational institutions are now immune to discrimination remains contestable. Social realities often defy the ostensible progress encapsulated in these legislative milestones. Although most people may not experience explicit discrimination, a subset of the population has experienced incidents that contradict this narrative of equality.

My own 2012 ordeal at a well-regarded American University serves as a stark illustration. Despite being a standard student with no exceptional needs, I faced what could only be described as a terrifying experience, one that shattered the illusion of an unbiased academic environment. Interestingly, I did not have avenues of redress against those who had subjected me to this ordeal. This unsettling experience, at least for me, serves as a powerful reminder that, despite legal advances, there remains a disturbing undercurrent of inequality and discrimination in American educational institutions.

The harrowing experience at the eminent university irrevocably altered my perception of the American educational system. This difficult period has left an indelible imprint on my mind. For those interested in an in-depth exploration of my specific ordeal, I have penned a comprehensive work titled *Studying While Black in America*, which I warmly invite you to peruse.[1]

It should be noted that my experience is not an isolated incident. Many have endured similar, if not more distressing, situations. A catalog of such incidents can be invaluable for those seeking to understand the complex web of challenges students face on university campuses across the United States.

To deepen your understanding, I point you to a selection of pivotal articles: 1) Levenson and Stapleton (2018, detailing how police were called by a black student at Yale University (Levenson & Stapleton, 2018); 2) Lockhart (2018), recounting an episode in which a professor called the police on a black student (Lockhart, 2018); and 3) Varkiani (2018), discussing an instance when the police were alerted because a black student was eating lunch in the common area of her university (Varkiani, 2018). Through these articles, one can

---

[1] The book is available on my website (www.benwoodjohnson, www.benwoodjbooks.com, www.teskopublishing.com) and in places where books are sold.

appreciate the intricate, but often unsettling, realities that pervade American educational institutions, particularly when it comes to adult education. For further elucidation and context, please refer to the *recommended readings* section toward the end of the document (on pages 83-84).

-2-

DEFINING THE TERM "ADULT EDUCATION"

Despite elucidating the complexities surrounding the world of adult education, one might still find the self grappling with lingering questions. The term "adult learning" appears simple on the surface but delves into intricate divergences upon closer examination. These divergences are often amplified by the fact that the very term "adult" carries various connotations for different individuals.

When asked about the definition of adult education, respondents often offer perspectives that may not align with the essence of the term. The scope of meanings people attribute to "adult learning" can fluctuate depending on individual life experiences, educational background, and social norms.

Knowles (1980) posits a tripartite conceptual framework for adult education. The first component is directly related to the learning processes that adults engage in (Knowles, 1980b, 1980a). The second component, as articulated by Knowles, encompasses a range of organized activities organized by educational institutions (Knowles, 1980b, 1980a). Lastly, Knowles further contends that adult education crystallizes these preceding components into a movement or a field of social practice (Knowles, 1980b, 1980a). In this way, the term "adult education" morphs into a multidimensional concept, an intricate network of processes, activities, and social engagements.

Based on Knowles' foundational framework, adult education could be argued to extend beyond institutionalized learning and social practice to infiltrate various sectors of life. It also intersects with issues of social justice, career advancement, and personal development. The labyrinth of adult learning is not only academic, but also experiential, often demanding a synthesis of formal instruction with life experiences.

Adult education refers to the process of providing educational opportunities and resources to adults beyond the traditional school age. It is a field of study that focuses on the unique needs and characteristics of adult learners (Wilson, 2012). Adult education can take various forms. These include formal instruction based on a classroom setting. Even so, online learning is another method. Vocational training is also a form of adult education. But community-based programs are another example.

An important aspect of adult education is the recognition of the adult learner as an active participant in the learning process. Adult learners bring their own experiences, knowledge, and motivations to the learning environment, which can influence their learning outcomes (Huang, 2002). Therefore, adult education often incorporates learner-centered approaches that emphasize active engagement, practical application, and relevance to real-life situations (Huang, 2002).

Another key consideration in adult education is the diversity of learners. Adult learners come from various backgrounds, with different levels of education, cultural experiences, and learning styles. As a result, adult education programs must be flexible and adaptable to meet the diverse needs of learners (Andersson et al., 2013). This process may involve the delivery of personalized instruction. It could also involve providing a variety of educational materials and resources; it requires the establishment of a supportive and inclusive learning environment (Boyadjieva & Ilieva-Trichkova, 2017).

The goals of adult education can vary depending on the specific context and needs of the learners. Some common goals include improving job skills and employability. Such goals must promote personal and professional development (Shen, 2022). Enhancing civic engagement and fostering lifelong learning are also important (Shen, 2022). Adult education can also play a role in addressing social issues and promoting social change. For example, it can contribute to social justice by providing educational opportunities to marginalized groups and promoting equity in access to education (Mas' ud & Imansari, 2022).

To design and deliver adult education programs effectively, educators and practitioners in the field must have a solid understanding of adult learning theories and instructional strategies. This includes knowledge of concepts such as constructivism, experiential learning, and brain-based learning, which can inform the design of effective instructional methods and materials (Angeliki & Loukas, 2021; Jang et al., 2021). Adult educators should have the skills and competencies necessary to simplify adult learning, such as communication, facilitation, and assessment (Tzovla & Kedraka, 2020).

Adult education is a field that recognizes the unique characteristics and needs of adult learners. It aims to provide them with educational opportunities and resources. It emphasizes learner-centered approaches, flexibility, and inclusion. Adult education can have various goals. It can include improving work skills. It can also promote personal development and address social issues. To be effective, adult education programs must be informed by adult learning theories, which must also be implemented by qualified and knowledgeable educators.

TECHNOLOGY AND ADULT EDUCATION

The advent of digital technologies and on-line platforms has further expanded the contours of adult education. Online courses, webinars, and workshops have revolutionized the availability of knowledge. They allow adults to participate in learning experiences that offer flexibility. These learning experiences are not restricted by geographical boundaries. These digital advances improve the conventional perspective of adult learning. They metamorphosize it into a global phenomenon. This singularity transcends physical and temporal constraints.

Adult education increasingly adopts an interdisciplinary approach. Today's adult learners often require a combination of hard skills, such as technological proficiency, and soft skills, such as effective communication. This holistic perspective enriches the learner, but also challenges educators to evolve their teaching methodologies. They need to develop curricula that are technically rigorous. These curricula should be emotionally resonant. This further complicates the complex realm of adult education.

The landscape of adult learning is in a dynamic flux. It is often influenced by technological advancements, social imperatives, and pedagogical innovations. It remains a domain not only of skill acquisition but also of cultural exchange, personal transformation, and even societal evolution.

In academic discourse, Knowles' conceptual framework for adult learning often faces rigorous scrutiny. Critics question its completeness and relevance. They propose alternative models that deviate from Knowles' perspective. For example, certain academics contend that Knowles' framework is excessively focused on western perspectives. They argue that it does not adequately consider the cultural subtleties of adult education in various global settings. They posit that adult learning is not a monolithic experience but a multifaceted phenomenon that varies according to cultural, social, and even economic conditions.

Another area of debate refers to the rigid demarcation between "adult" and "traditional" learners. Observers in psychology and developmental studies have questioned this binary classification. They proposed that learning is a continuous process; it extends from childhood to old age. Therefore, the demarcation that distinguishes an adult learner from a conventional one might be less rigid than previously believed. This contradicts the distinct stages that Knowles proposes.

The rise of informal learning environments, such as community centers and online forums, has muddled the clarity of what constitutes organized educational activities. Critics argue that Knowles' emphasis on institutionally organized learning overlooks the importance of these less formal settings, which have proven to be critical in the development of skills and lifelong learning.

Although the discussion outline in this compilation does not intend to resolve these conflicts, it serves to highlight the divergent perspectives that make the discourse on adult learning rich and contested. Differences in academic perspectives highlight the complexity of the topic. This suggests that one singular definition may not be enough to fully encompass its diverse aspects.

AN ELUSIVE SEARCH FOR DEFINITION

The concept of adult education constitutes a perplexing labyrinth within the American educational system. Navigating through this intricate web offers no definitive answers, only a series of questions that perpetuate the enigma. Thus, it becomes evident that the idea of adult learning remains shattered by a cloud of ambiguity that even experts find difficult to pierce.

Vaske (2001) contended that the field of adult learning is elusive. It is plagued by a multitude of conflicting objectives and interpretations (Vaske, 2001). These disparities stem from kaleidoscopic perspectives on who adult learners are and what characteristics they bring to the educational setting. The subject of adult learning sits in relative obscurity within the broader educational landscape. One may rightfully inquire as to the underlying causes of this lack of scholarly attention.

Attempting to pinpoint a precise reason for this scholarly neglect proves to be a Herculean task. A plausible hypothesis could be the presumption that adult learners inherently possess self-efficacy and direction. Education administrators often work in the belief that adult students traverse educational routes with a higher degree of maturity and self-direction. Consequently, there is less academic emphasis on this demographic. This scenario denotes that adult education is saturated with complexities. This reality calls for more academic exploration to uncover the truths that are hidden beneath layers of assumptions and speculation.

Educators, including teachers and university professors, often do not pay much attention to adult learners. They operate under the assumption that these mature students can navigate the academic landscape with inherent self-reliance. A prevailing sentiment, although one that may be misconstrued, is that older learners do not necessitate the same degree of academic oversight as their younger counterparts. Here, the focus is on younger individuals, particularly those who have recently embarked on their college journey away from the protective environment of the home.

The juxtaposition between younger and older adult learners reveals palpable advantages in favor of the former group. Conventional wisdom and educational metrics often show that younger learners outperform older adults in academic settings. This advantage manifests itself not only in quantifiable metrics but also in socio-cultural dynamics that create an educational climate more congenial to younger adults.

Such discrepancies between younger and older adult learners are not merely academic; they permeate the fabric of everyday life and underscore broader social assumptions. The challenges faced by older adults in academic settings serve as a microcosm of larger questions surrounding age, competence, and societal expectations. The comparative disadvantages faced by older learners extend far beyond classrooms and syllabi. These disadvantages warrant a comprehensive investigation and discussion.

A UNIVERSAL APPROACH

In academic circles, the term adult education encompasses a wide range of learning stages: elementary, secondary, and post-secondary education. The concept is not limited to these stages. It also targets people who have aged beyond what society classifies as "traditional students." According to a modern conceptualization by UNESCO, adult education aims to improve technical or professional qualifications, further develop abilities, and enrich knowledge with the purpose of completing a level of formal education, or to gain knowledge, skills, and competencies in a new field, or to refresh or update their knowledge in a particular field. This also includes what can be referred to as "continuing education," "recurrent education," or "second chance education" (UNESCO, 2017).

The preceding assessment of the nature of adult education posits that adult learners exhibit an elevated level of independence. Such learners often arrive at educational institutions with a well-defined sense of purpose. They exhibit distinct expectations from the educational process and reveal a willingness to dive into the learning experience. These mature students also show significant motivation. This prepares them for intensive academic participation.

This preconceived notion of independence and motivation among adult learners is intriguing, as it challenges educators to reevaluate their pedagogical strategies. While these mature students bring a variety of life experiences to the classroom, they also bring unique academic needs. Hence, the issue extends beyond simple presumptions and infiltrates deeper questions concerning the effectiveness of current educational paradigms in catering to this demographically complex group. Is our education system adequately equipped to meet the diverse and nuanced needs of adult learners? This question merits serious scholarly consideration.

In scholarly discourse, the terms "higher education" and "adult education" are often used interchangeably. However, a closer examination reveals distinct nuances. From a semantic point of view, these terms differ significantly in their implications and applicability. While "higher education" refers to a formal learning process that culminates in the achievement of academic degrees, "adult education" encompasses a broader and more inclusive range of learning experiences aimed at mature learners.

In this book, it is worthy of note, both terms are employed in a fluid manner. Yet, each concept retains its specific connotation. This choice of diction serves as more than a rhetorical flourish; it emphasizes the complex realities of these two educational frameworks. As you read the document, I invite you to keep an open mind. The issues that dominate the debate on higher education and higher education are neither superficial nor static; they are dynamic, constantly shaped, and reshaped by evolving societal, economic, and technological factors. These complexities make it imperative to approach the subject matter with both intellectual rigor and interpretive flexibility.

While the preceding sections have illuminated the differences between adult education and higher education, there are additional layers that deserve scholarly attention. One such layer is the impact of life circumstances on adult learners. Unlike their younger counterparts, adult students often balance responsibilities such as full-time employment, family commitments, and even elder care. These responsibilities do not serve as background noise; they exert a significant influence on the adult learning experience. This affects everything. It influences class participation. It also affects the application of new knowledge.

Another critical dimension worth exploring is the role of technology in adult education. The rapid pace of technological advancements does not only affect traditional classroom settings. For adult learners, the digital realm often serves as both a facilitator and a barrier. On the one hand, online courses and digital resources can make education more accessible to those who cannot attend traditional classes. In contrast, a digital divide is also present, if not too pervasive at times. It affects individuals who lack either technological literacy or the resources. Their full participation in a digitally mediated educational environment is impeded.

Let us consider institutional perspectives on adult education. Academic institutions, policymakers, and employers often view adult education through different lenses. For academic institutions, adult education represents an opportunity for enrollment growth and diversification. For policymakers, it is a chance to reskill the workforce, thus boosting economic productivity. Employers, meanwhile, often see adult education as a pathway to upskilling their employees, although they may have concerns about return on investment. These diverse perspectives influence policy and practice. They also contribute to the multifaceted and nuanced nature of adult education as a field of study.

A POLICY STREAM

-3-

NEW TRENDS IN EDUCATION

Amid a sea change in the educational landscape, an emerging trend captures scholarly and public attention alike: the primacy of educational standards. Fueled by globalization, the ascendancy of a market economy, and relentless technological innovation, there has emerged a fervent demand for a workforce with specialized skills. Despite its apparent simplicity, this change in thinking engenders complex debates, especially around the qualifications that define a skilled worker.

A pressing issue in this discourse revolves around a narrowing conception of what makes up a skilled worker. In contemporary contexts, the baseline criteria for skilled work now often extend beyond mere experience or job readiness; they demand formal educational qualifications. By tradition, to acquire recognition as a skilled worker, one usually needs a college degree or specialized technical training. This evolution underscores that the complexities involved in higher education often escape cursory observation and deserve rigorous scrutiny.

A notable repercussion of these shifting standards is the migration of traditional workers back to educational institutions. The era when a high school diploma or a General Educational Development (GED) certificate sufficed for secure employment has irreversibly ended. In today's competitive job market, experience in isolation does not guarantee job placement. A college degree or a technical certification has increasingly become a de facto prerequisite even for entering job interviews.

The practical ramifications of this educational shift are both stark and widespread. Individuals with only high school education are progressively sidelined in the job market. Although it is true that high-paying jobs remain competitive, it is imperative to recognize that such opportunities have also become increasingly scarce. This intensification of educational and skill prerequisites presents an urgent issue that warrants scholarly exploration and societal intervention.

In the context of a constrained job market, or more precisely the volatile nature of contemporary labor dynamics, employers have become exceedingly discerning in their hiring processes. Securing meaningful employment with limited educational or skill-based qualifications has become obsolete. To put it bluntly, the absence of relevant skills makes the task of finding decent employment extraordinarily challenging, if not utterly implausible.

The importance of having the correct amalgamation of skills, relevant training, and pertinent credentials cannot be overstated. These factors have evolved into nonnegotiable prerequisites for job seekers aiming to secure stable and well-compensated positions. In such an environment, the casual job seeker or the minimally qualified individual faces steep barriers to entry into the labor market.

This intense selectivity of employers amplifies the urgency for potential employees to not only obtain but excel in specialized training and education. In a labor market characterized by its fragility, the burden of adaptability and continuous skill acquisition falls disproportionately on the job seeker. Thus, it becomes crucial for academic and vocational institutions to re-evaluate and adapt their curricula to better prepare their students for the harsh realities of a fiercely competitive and rapidly evolving job market.

EXPERIENCE AND EMPLOYMENT

Contrary to widespread belief that field-specific experience serves as a golden ticket to gainful employment, the intricate reality of the labor market often refutes this notion. One could argue that the exclusive reliance on experience does not guarantee a lucrative job in today's complex employment landscape. Multiple variables come into play, such as educational background, specialization, and the institution where training was performed, be it a trade school or a university.

Employers overwhelmingly prioritize a specific criterion when considering new hires, particularly for entry-level positions within numerous American corporations. This criterion is the possession of a college degree that aligns with the immediate needs of the organization. This almost universal requirement highlights the essential importance that employers attach to formal education. They consider it an absolute must for prospective candidates.

Faced with an inexorable labor market, job seekers are left without alternatives but to accept these stringent demands. Economic realities often compel people to return to academia or to pursue advanced degrees. Over the past few decades, the cost of living has increased significantly, while wages have remained stagnant. Securing employment that offers financial stability becomes not just an aspiration, but an absolute necessity for survival. For most, the path to such a stable job, sometimes even the job of one's dreams, unavoidably passes through the hallowed halls of a reputable educational institution.

Earning a college degree is undeniably a labor-intensive endeavor. It requires a substantial investment of time. It also requires effort and resources. Individuals must navigate a labyrinthine educational landscape, overcome academic hurdles, and meet rigorous standards to attain the coveted academic credential. Given this complexity, the argument can be made that the path to graduation presents formidable challenges for a significant subset of the population.

Achieving the status of a college graduate remains an elusive goal for many. Although aspirations may be high, completion rates show that a lesser proportion of people successfully traverse the educational odyssey. This underscores the imperative to examine the underlying factors that contribute to this shortfall, whether they are systemic barriers or personal circumstances, and to strategize effective interventions to improve this trend.

EARNING A COLLEGE DEGREE

Attaining a college degree has long been a hallmark of success, a tangible manifestation of individual prowess and economic prosperity. This academic credential serves not only as an emblem of personal achievement, but also as a stepping-stone to upward mobility in society. The allure of the title "college graduate" exerts a compelling influence on people across generations, and its value in social and economic capital endures.

Returning to the academic sphere often becomes a compelling necessity for many, particularly older adults, who face stagnation in their professional trajectories. No longer does prior experience alone suffice to secure lucrative positions or foster career progression. Faced with a progressively competitive job market, older learners often feel obligated to return to the world of academia. They begin the path to acquire modern skills that are considered essential by the market. This endeavor often unfolds as a Sisyphean struggle, with many succumbing to the challenges that hinder their educational pursuit.

For this cohort of learners, especially those who do not live on campus, the logistical challenges of attending a university further complicate their educational journey. Commuting to and from the institution while managing their existing responsibilities magnifies the complexity of their academic endeavors. Therefore, for adults who juggle family duties, full-time employment, and other obligations, the barriers to higher education extend beyond the purely academic. Therefore, the allure of career progression motivates them to view higher education as a potential path. However, the truth of their life situations frequently acts as impediments. This turns the consideration of returning to school into a complex and multifaceted decision.

Choosing the right educational institution is another dilemma for older adults. This challenge further complicates their path back to academia. Although community colleges and technical schools might offer more accessible routes, the allure of a university education often proves irresistible. This predilection for universities comes from the prestige traditionally associated with such institutions. What most adult learners discover, often to their detriment, is that the conventional educational setting of a university does not necessarily cater to their unique needs and circumstances.

In their quest for professional improvement, adult learners often turn to higher education as the fulcrum for acquiring essential competencies for a turbulent job market. However, choosing the university path presents its own set of formidable challenges that can inhibit its academic and professional progression. Universities, especially those in the United States, are not always designed with the older student in mind. Age-related biases, an overwhelming focus on traditional-aged students, and a less-than-flexible curriculum can make universities a hostile environment for the adult learner.

Financial considerations further compound the obstacles facing adult learners. American universities, far from being benevolent educational sanctuaries, often operate as for-profit enterprises. The soaring tuition costs put an additional strain on older adults, many of whom already manage a myriad of financial responsibilities. In certain instances, the exploitative tendencies of some institutions compound this problem. They lead adult learners into a vicious cycle of debt. They leave these learners with unfulfilled academic aspirations. Thus, navigating the American educational landscape becomes a precarious endeavor for adult learners, fraught with economic, logistic, and institutional challenges.

In the complex ecosystem of higher education, the quest for revenue can undeniably play a significant role, especially with adult learners. Although not every institution employs the same financial model, universities levy higher tuition fees compared to their community college or technical school counterparts. The financial burden can serve as a substantial deterrent for adult learners considering a return to academic life.

The intellectual rigor found in many universities can pose its own set of challenges to adult learners. This increased academic intensity often converges with other life commitments, such as work and family, to create a strenuous learning environment. Under such conditions, the educational experience, far from being an enlightening journey, can metamorphose into an oppressive ordeal for older students.

Adult learners must negotiate a labyrinth of financial, intellectual, and logistical challenges when selecting their educational path. The potentially excessive costs, combined with the rigorous academic demands, can transform what should be an enriching experience into a burdensome undertaking. Therefore, as adult learners weigh their options, they must be aware of both the explicit and hidden costs associated with higher learning, as well as the academic rigor they will encounter.

CHALLENGES FOR ADULT LEARNERS

The landscape of adult learning is teeming with complexities, especially in categorizing who exactly qualifies as "adult learner." Age, often presumed to be a clear delineator, is less precise than one might think. Individuals pursuing education later in life may escape easy categorization; they may not conform to specific age-related or socioeconomic expectations. Thus, one finds a list of individuals whose ages, goals, and economic conditions defy simple classification.

The demographic composition of adult learners is far from homogeneous. This leads to frequent misinterpretations of what adult education truly encapsulates. While age differences between students can introduce an element of similarity or dissimilarity, they cannot offer a comprehensive understanding of the identities of adult learners. Age alone does not suffice as the sole criterion for including or exclusion from this diverse group.

The concept of adulthood itself presents a minefield of ambiguities. Typically, people over the age of twenty-five earn the "adult" label. This neat numerical cut-off belies the more nuanced reality observed in educational settings. A range of definitions for adulthood extends beyond this age-centric model. This results in continuing inconsistencies. Even within the age-based model, considerable disparities can emerge in terms of the traits people ascribe to those called "adult learners." The task of defining an adult learner remains an intricate undertaking rife with subjective interpretations and inconsistent criteria.

The prevalent misconceptions about adult learning further complicate the task of clearly identifying who falls under the umbrella term "adult learner." These misconceptions pose significant challenges in developing educational programs that meet the unique needs of this diverse group. In fact, creating a universally suitable educational framework becomes an increasingly complex endeavor given the multifaceted nature of adult learning.

Various stereotypes and preconceptions characterize what many perceive as adult learning, though a comprehensive exploration of all existing labels would be beyond the scope of this discussion. Nonetheless, some dominant perspectives merit closer examination. For example, certain analysts consider adult education from a gender perspective. They investigate how varying expectations for men and women influence their learning experiences. Others view race as a critical component. They examine how racial and ethnic identities shape educational opportunities. They also investigated how these identities affect outcomes.

Another group emphasizes socioeconomic status as a critical defining factor. They investigate the role of financial resources in one's educational journey. They also scrutinize how social capital contributes to this journey.

Each of these perspectives offers its own set of challenges and opportunities, and each contributes to the broader and more nuanced picture of what adult learning entails. In sum, adult learning is not a monolithic experience, but rather a rich, complex interplay of several factors that defy easy categorization or simplistic solutions.

Adult education extends far beyond the commonly discussed parameters of race, gender, and socioeconomic status. Various additional factors play crucial roles in shaping the adult learning experience, many of which often escape attention in mainstream discourse. Among these overlooked elements, pedagogical approaches, employment commitments, challenges of single parenthood, language barriers, and cultural nuances each introduce their own set of complexities.

Pedagogical strategies, the argument can be made, can profoundly affect the adult learning experience. Adults typically benefit from experiential learning, where real-world application of knowledge improves retention and understanding. The interplay between employment and education presents another major concern. Most adult learners must balance taxing work schedules with their educational obligations. This situation raises questions about the ideal format and timing of adult education programs.

Single parenthood brings an additional layer of complexity, as these learners must also negotiate childcare responsibilities while attending classes or completing coursework. Language barriers often present unique challenges, particularly for those whose first language is not the medium of instruction. Cultural factors also play a significant role in learning. They can facilitate or hinder the process. This depends on the ability of educational institutions to adapt their programs appropriately. They need to consider diverse norms and expectations.

These issues warrant close examination in any robust discussion of adult education, as they contribute to a more intricate and nuanced understanding of the adult learner's experience. Ignoring these factors risks perpetuating incomplete or distorted views, doing a disservice to efforts aimed at improving adult educational outcomes.

-4-

ASSESSING POLICY ISSUES

In the United States, the authority over education lies with individual states. Intriguingly, the guiding policy framework for adult education often originates in the federal sphere. This duality ignites intense discourse. It often stimulates inquiries about the degree to which federal intervention in education affairs is necessary. It also raises questions about the legitimacy of such actions.

Although the U.S. Constitution does not explicitly grant the federal government authority over education, historical instances show that federal involvement in educational matters, particularly in adult education, is far from unprecedented. Take, for instance, the groundbreaking GI Bill enacted in 1944. According to the U.S. Department of Veteran Affairs, this transformative legislation facilitated higher education and vocational training for millions of returning war veterans. Similarly, as Travers (2013) highlights, in 1948, the federal government broadened its educational obligations toward veterans. This action highlighted a recurring pattern of federal intervention in education-related issues.

The National Literacy Act of 1991 marks another watershed moment in adult education policy. This groundbreaking legislation paved the way for the Adult Education Act, which, in turn, was superseded by the Workforce Investment Act of 1998. These legislative landmarks unveil an intriguing path of federal participation. They underscore the ability of the federal government to pioneer new perspectives in adult education policy. While this federal-state interplay continues to be a subject of debate, it is evident that federal legislation has played and continues to play a transformative role in shaping the contours of adult education in the United States.

The National Adult Education Professional Development Consortium records that a plethora of legislation concerning adult education was enacted by the federal government between 1964 and 1998. Most notably, the Clinton administration spearheaded the Workforce Investment Act (WIA) in 1998, a milestone that became instrumental in shaping adult education policies across numerous states (Milana & McBain, 2014). To facilitate the effective implementation of the WIA, the federal government even established a specialized division for adult education and literacy (U.S. Department of Education, 2013). These legislative actions reveal a concerted federal effort to support adult education initiatives.

A cornerstone of these policies was the focus on improving literacy for adult learners. Financial aid was channeled at the state level to propel a variety of educational efforts. These efforts included, but were not limited to, evening schools tailored for adults, part-time educational programs, and even citizenship classes (U.S. Department of Education, 2003). The overarching ambition was to provide diverse and meaningful educational opportunities to adults, thus addressing the literacy gap and equipping them with the necessary life skills. In doing so, the federal government demonstrated its commitment to elevating the standard and scope of adult education.

The U.S. Department of Education (2005) indicated that the newly enacted legislation aimed at streamlining processes of adult education. It is was important to do so across federal employment, adult education, and vocational rehabilitation programs (U.S. Department of Education, 2005b). These legislative landmarks unveil an intriguing path of federal participation. They underscore the ability of the federal government to pioneer new perspectives in adult education policy. This goal, though broad, has led to ongoing debates surrounding the exact definition of the term "adult learner." While the policies lay a foundation, they also opened the Pandora's box of questions that dove into the intricacies of the individuals who precisely qualify for this designation. It is essential, therefore, to examine these contestations and complexities in greater detail to arrive at a more nuanced understanding of the adult learner in the context of American educational policy.

BEING AN ADULT LEARNER

The question of who precisely qualifies as an adult learner proves to be a particularly contentious issue, especially when observed through the lens of policy formulation. Although adults are the primary recipients of specially designed educational policies for them, the definition of "adult" remains ambiguous. Likewise, the Workforce Investment Act of 1998 includes within its purview not only middle-aged individuals but also people under the age of 21. This broad categorization complicates efforts to determine a target population with cohesive characteristics and shared values.

Schneider and Ingram (1993) posited that school officials must create relevant policies. With policymaking, public officials can focus keenly on power dynamics, social constructs, and public pressure to create policies that are both relevant and effective (Schneider & Ingram, 1993). In adult education, these social constructs carry significantly less weight. The target population in question lacks powerful values, symbols, or images that define their unique characteristics. Therefore, it becomes an intricate endeavor to frame policies that would benefit this group in a cohesive way.

Adding to the mentioned complexity, adult education transcends the traditional bounds of adult basic education and is not confined solely to the purview of state departments of education (U.S. Department of Education, 2005a, 2005b). This expansion of scope makes the task of identifying the real beneficiaries of adult education policies even more challenging. As a result, a concrete response to the question of who should genuinely benefit from policies intended for adult education remains elusive. This encourages more scholarly investigation and discussion.

Observers have noted a sense of neglect among policymakers in addressing adult educational issues. One factor that may contribute to this phenomenon is the low level of voter participation among college students, who are adult learners. The reduced political influence of this group means that they rarely shape politics at both local and national levels. This lack of influence allows public officials the latitude to craft policies that may not directly meet the specific needs or interests of adult learners in higher education institutions.

Scholarly research over the past decades has delved into the relationship between voter participation and policy formulation (Schneider & Ingram, 1993). The consensus appears to suggest that the impact of adult education on community participation and, by extension, on policymaking remains marginal. Adult learners do not constitute a homogenous or unified demographic with political weight. Their lack of political significance means that they exert a minimal influence on both local and national policies. Consequently, adult learners do not constitute an important constituency; they are not a force that can drive the public discourse, which could lead to substantial policy changes in education.

Adult educational policies often fail to address the specific needs of adult learners. The lack of interest in adult education and the meager political weight adult learners represent suggest a glaring gap in policy design in adult educational policies, one that underscores the need for a more nuanced understanding of the adult learner population and its diverse needs. It serves as an invitation for further research and discussion to examine how this gap could be filled effectively to the benefit of adult learners and society at large.

MAKING ADULT EDUCATION POLICIES

In adult education, identifying the primary architects of relevant policies presents a complex challenge. Although the federal government undeniably wields considerable influence in establishing overarching educational directives, the nuance and specificity in policy execution often fall within the authority of local officials. Besides the federal government, local entities often play a role in forming regulations related to adult learners. This adds complexity to the landscape of policymaking.

The theoretical framework of the social construction of target populations, as delineated by Schneider and Ingram (1993), offers valuable insights into this dynamic. They posited that certain groups enjoy an advantage in policy formulation because of their socio-political positioning. In the specific context of adult education, the demographic in question rarely exerts enough political influence on influencing policymakers' decisions. This absence of political repercussions for the officials in charge makes the group almost invisible in policy considerations.

Although adult education is an important aspect of the American educational system, as it is the foundation of higher education, it has not yet captured the broad public attention that would compel immediate action from elected officials. Schneider and Ingram (1993) suggested that policymakers often remain indifferent to constituencies that lack the power to affect their political future. When the potential impact of a group on reelection remains marginal, elected officials may neglect to engage in the nuanced social construction of target populations. Therefore, the issue of adult education continues to linger in the shadows, deprived of the focused, responsive policymaking it so desperately requires.

In the labyrinthine context of adult education policy, a striking factor is the absence of a unified characteristic that makes the target population a prominent social entity. This lack of clarity and focus inevitably weakens the eligibility criteria for adult education programs. They become a complex mixture of race, gender, occupational status, and income level. Given this absence of a unified framework, benefits are allocated based on a disparate set of reasons, each of which has its own weight in decision-making.

Another layer of complexity emerges when contrasting the behaviors and attitudes of older and younger adult learners. Older adults often show a higher level of responsibility and caution in their educational endeavors. In stark contrast to their younger counterparts, they often avoid accruing debilitating educational debt. Their prudent strategy often includes obtaining government funding. They also make use of state-funded programs to cover tuition fees. This reveals a unique pattern of dependence on existing systems for educational financing.

In contrast, younger learners often approach tertiary education with less fiscal prudence, often accumulating substantial debt for a college degree. Their commitment to academic rigor may vary. This can create a disparity in focus and discipline compared to older adults. Such contrasting attitudes toward education and financial commitment further complicate the policy landscape. They reveal that a one-size-fits-all approach to adult education policy would be insufficient. It could even be problematic. As a result, the priorities and incentives that guide educational policies for these two distinct demographic groups may differ significantly. This situation calls for subtle strategies. However, these strategies must address the divergent needs of adult learners.

An often overlooked but pivotal element in the discourse on adult education is the role of technological literacy. Although policy discussions frequently focus on traditional forms of literacy, the rapid digitalization of society places technological literacy at the forefront of modern education. Older adults, who have grown up in a less digitally saturated environment, often face steep learning curves when adapting to modern technologies. This technological gap not only affects their employability, but also poses a barrier to accessing educational resources that have changed online.

On the other side of the spectrum, young adults exhibit a contrasting dilemma. Often digitally savvy, they face information overload and the potential erosion of critical thinking skills. The digital landscape offers a wealth of information but lacks the curatorial functions traditionally provided by educational institutions. This situation raises questions about the adaptability and relevance of current adult education policies, which may not adequately address these emerging challenges.

The spatial dimensions of adult education warrant attention. Geographic disparities often influence the availability and quality of educational resources. Rural areas may lack the infrastructure necessary for high-speed internet access, which may prevent participation in online courses. In addition, urban environments can offer a multitude of educational opportunities, but are often marred by excessive living costs and transportation issues. Therefore, the geographic context impacts the efficiency and reachability of adult education programs. This adds a layer of complexity to an issue that is already multidimensional.

A PEDAGOGICAL STREAM

-5-

EXPLORING EDUCATIONAL ISSUES

Adult education became a deeply personal issue for me. It illuminated its intricate complexity. Engaging in this topic as an adult learner allowed me to perceive the intricacies of the educational process in a new light. In my youth, I would say, I often found myself amused by older individuals, such as my mother or my neighbor, who attended night classes.

This early fascination was tinged with a touch of irony; I already knew the educational hurdles they would face. But what I did not understand at that point was the distinct educational experience that awaited adult learners. Unlike children or even younger adults, who often endure punitive measures for misconduct, adult learners engage in an environment uniquely tailored to their needs and life circumstances.

My experience back then is not that different from the nature of public perceptions vis-à-vis adult education nowadays. The public often misinterprets the scope of adult learning. As outlined earlier, the common belief is that adult learners are independent. However, this view reflects a common misunderstanding about adult education. It also suggests that all adult learners are older individuals.

Another misconception is that adult learners are individuals who returned to school for the first time or as part of a life transition. This concept is fundamentally mistaken. Adult learners are not necessarily adults in the true sense of the term. They represent a wide range of individuals from various age groups. For instance, adult learners may include people in their early twenties.

They may also include individuals who are deep into their golden years and even in their late fifties and beyond. So, the idea that all adults are the same often creates incommensurable issues, which few educators are prepared to navigate.

When it comes to instructing adults, for instance, there is a debate as to which teaching style best fits adults, as opposed to younger individuals, including children. In this case, pedagogical approaches suitable for children or young adults often prove inadequate for this diverse cohort (i.e., older adults). Thus, educators and policymakers often find it necessary to draw a clear delineation between the two groups. For instance, they must consider the unique attributes and needs of adult learners to design effective and age-appropriate teaching strategies.

In various educational settings, the pedagogical needs of adult learners, particularly older persons, often go unaddressed. This issue often raises several pressing questions, which warrant careful consideration for the advancement of higher education as a whole. Among the salient questions worthy of further clarifications, we ask the following: How can the system rectify the glaring problems that pervade the educational landscape for adult learners? What options do adult learners have when faced with unjust treatment? Do educators have specific responsibilities for older adults in their classrooms? But do educational institutions owe duties to nontraditional learners?

Granted, these questions do not have straightforward answers. The pursuit of solutions often delves into subjective realms. This complicates the search for strategies that can be universally applied. However, engaging in a rigorous discourse can illuminate the paths to remediation, some of which may appear technical, but essential.

As potential solutions, educational institutions should implement a curriculum specifically designed for adult learners. Such an initiative could address the unique cognitive, emotional, and life-stage needs of this demographic. In the same way, avenues of redress should be open and accessible for adults who experience unfair treatment. Establishing an ombudsman service or a grievance committee within the educational setting might serve this purpose effectively.

Moreover, professors and teachers must recognize the different learning styles and needs of older adults. They must incorporate adult learning theories into their teaching methodologies. It is the responsibility of educational institutions to foster inclusive learning environments. Providing flexible schedules is a way to cater to non-traditional learners. It is recommended that they provide personalized career services. They should also provide lifelong learning opportunities.

When these multifaceted avenues are examined, the debate is closer to yielding tangible responses to the issues that adult learners generally face in their pursuit of an education. Adopting the recommended approaches can lead to actionable solutions. These solutions, in turn, can better serve this adult learning demographic, which may improve the educational experience of this constituency within the realm of education.

PEDAGOGY VERSUS ANDRAGOGY

To reiterate a previous point at issue in the debate: what is the best teaching style to address adult learner needs? The answer is not clear-cut. But from the point of view of educational theory, two distinct teaching styles have emerged as particularly salient: pedagogy and andragogy.

The first teaching style, known as pedagogy, has roots deep within traditional educational systems. The second style, termed andragogy, became more popular as educators recognized the unique requirements of adult learners. Although both styles have been subject to extensive scholarly scrutiny, the debate continues which approach best serves the needs of adult learners.

It would be erroneous to claim that there is a one-size-fits-all teaching model that universally addresses the learning styles of all demographic groups. In fact, adult learners present a complex and dynamic educational profile that defies easy categorization. Educational theorists, practitioners, and policymakers continue to grapple with a fundamental question. Which teaching model should prevail to offer the most effective educational experience for adults?

Some proponents argue that andragogy, known for its focus on self-directed learning and practical application of knowledge, provides the optimal framework for adult education. This view gains particular traction in higher education settings, where the emphasis often leans toward critical thinking and critical thinking skills. On the contrary, there are scholars who posit that pedagogy, with its structured environment and teacher-directed approach, might still offer valuable learning experiences for adults.

The question of which teaching style reigns supreme for adult learners remains a subject of intellectual debate. In fact, there is not a clear winner. But as educational paradigms continue to evolve, so will perspectives on how best to serve this diverse and intricate demographic of learners.

In educational practice, the line demarcating the pedagogical and andragogical approaches often blurs, despite their theoretical distinctions. Although the present edition does not plunge into the intricacies of each teaching style, it aims to illuminate their complexities through various lenses. To foster a more nuanced understanding, it becomes essential to probe these methodologies in greater depth.

Pedagogy traditionally adheres to a top-down, teacher-centered model, in which the educator disseminates knowledge, and the learners absorb it in a structured setting. Andragogy, in contrast, embraces a more collaborative, learner-centered framework that encourages self-directed learning and the application of knowledge in real-world contexts. In practice, elements of both models often intertwine. This leads to hybrid teaching styles that draw on the strengths of each approach.

The intricate blend of these models in the classroom creates fertile grounds for scholarly investigation. The fact that pedagogy and andragogy can converge in practice opens up a fascinating realm of possibilities. It pushes us to question (continually, of course) how these approaches can coalesce into a more effective educational experience for learners of all ages, particularly adults, whose needs often differ. To say is again, as the landscape of education continues to evolve, these inquiries will certainly contribute valuable insights into how we can optimize the educational journey for diverse learner populations.

TEACHING ADULTS

When confronting the intricacies of adult education, a variety of challenges emerge. Pedagogical approaches, traditionally used to educate children, exhibit limitations when applied to mature learners, especially in higher education settings (Peterson, 2018). It invites us to question whether pedagogical methodologies truly resonate with the adult populace, whose educational needs sharply diverge from those of younger students.

Andragogy emerges as an alternative, defining itself as the "art and science of helping adults learn" (Peterson, 2018). Specifically, it focuses on facilitating older adults' educational experiences. Despite its apparent suitability, several issues warrant further examination. The question centers on the most effective method for instructing adults, particularly those of a younger age, in college settings. The academic community remains divided; no unambiguous solutions have accumulated in this ongoing discourse.

The elusive nature of the term "adult education" could underpin this impasse. The terminology itself contains unformulated definitions, further obfuscating the debate. Differences between younger and older adults in educational settings often become indistinct. This makes clear categorizations difficult to achieve. The boundary between the educational needs of these different age groups is often unclear. This adds another layer of complexity to an already intricate issue.

Although I abstain from making claims regarding similarities or differences in learning skills between younger and older adults in the present dialogue, it is irrefutable that there are varied learning needs between age groups. For example, Green (1998) noted a difference between adult learning and other learners. The author posited that the ways in which adults learn differ significantly from the learning patterns of younger individuals (Green, 1998). These discrepancies not only challenge the uniform application of pedagogical or andragogical approaches, but also beckon further scholarly investigation. As educational paradigms continue to evolve, a deeper understanding of these divergent needs will undoubtedly guide and inform more effective and nuanced teaching strategies.

Besides physical distinctions, cognitive and psychological differences manifest between younger and older adults, potentially affecting their educational ability. For example, adult learners often actively seek learning experiences to navigate life transitions. Younger individuals, conversely, may not perceive the imperative nature of their educational journey, thus marking adult education as more voluntary than the often-compulsory education of the young.

This voluntarism leads to the following assumption. That is, adult learners are highly invested in their educational pursuits. Many believe that these learners allocate considerable time and resources to achieve their academic goals. However, this perspective only partially captures the nuanced realities of adult education. The enthusiasm and investment ascribed to adult learners often deviate from what transpires in actual educational settings.

In higher learning institutions, adult learners often encounter treatment that is incongruous with their age and life experience. In certain cases, older people find themselves in situations where their maturity is undermined. They are treated as if they were children.

On the contrary, sometimes expectations swing to the other extreme. The term "adult learner" is fraught with ambiguity, which further intensifies these inconsistencies. This makes it challenging to determine (conclusively, of course) who exactly falls under this classification. This lack of clarity not only muddles academic debates but also has tangible repercussions for the design and implementation of educational strategies tailored to addressing adult learner needs.

Navigating the labyrinthine landscape of adult education often proves more complicated than assumed. Older adults face significant obstacles in their pursuit of higher education. This situation prompts us to wonder if these barriers are intentionally constructed. These obstacles are not just academic; they often spill over into personal realms, further complicating the educational journey.

Adult learners often face significant obstacles. These obstacles impede their academic progress. The balance between school responsibilities and other life commitments poses a substantial challenge. Most people balance family obligations with full-time jobs and other personal matters while continuing their education. It becomes difficult to allocate time to academic activities.

The personal challenges faced by adult learners often infiltrate the educational environment, further exacerbating their struggles. Financial burdens, health concerns, and emotional stress can serve as additional obstacles, collectively painting a picture of adult education that is rife with complexity and fraught with challenges. These cumulative obstacles underscore the need to re-evaluate current frameworks and approaches to adult education.

TRADITIONAL VERSUS NONTRADITIONAL STUDENTS

The line separating young and old adults within educational settings remains ambiguous. More research is needed to clarify this vague division. Although older people have become more prevalent in academic settings, a comprehensive understanding of the characteristics that define adult learners remains lacking. Questions linger not only about traditional learners but also about nontraditional learners in these settings.

Emerging trends in higher education require a change in perspective. Investigations conducted by the Council for Adult and Experiential Learning (CAEL) have revealed a notable shift in the demographics of higher education (CAEL, 2000). According to their findings, approximately 60% of students engaged in higher education are of the non-traditional variety, with around 43% aged 25 years or older (CAEL, 2000). Enrollments of students 35 years and older witnessed an increase of 65% between 1985 and 1996 (CAEL, 2000). This could lead to a persistent upward trajectory.

These statistical revelations require a re-evaluation of conventional wisdom about college demographics. The archetype of the traditional college student, once characterized as an individual between 18- and 23-years old living in a campus dormitory, is no longer applicable. These days are now in the past. The modern landscape of higher education presents a much more nuanced portrait, with older adults making up a considerable proportion of the student body.

The composition of adult learners continues to resist a simple classification. They display a wide range of attributes. These attributes vary from age to gender to ethnicity. Although the composition of adult learners varies, they are not simply an older iteration of their traditional counterparts. This diverse community requires customized educational strategies. It places the responsibility on academic institutions to adapt and evolve.

The notion that adult learners exercise complete control over their educational path is often more idealistic than factual. Despite the widespread belief that adult learners are fully engaged in their educational pursuits, empirical evidence suggests a different narrative. Challenges pose a significant obstacle to their journey toward higher education. These challenges often include financial constraints. Family responsibilities also hinder their progress. All these factors collectively undermine the concept of complete control.

The popular conception of adult learners as self-directed and empowered ignores the systemic barriers they face. Most adult learners have multiple roles, such as parenting or full-time employment, which complicates their academic commitments. The restrictions imposed by these external responsibilities can inhibit their ability to focus solely on academic pursuits. This renders the idea of full control illusory.

Contrary to optimistic perceptions, the reality of adult education is fraught with difficulties that extend beyond individual control. Adult learners often navigate a labyrinthine educational system that may not be geared to their unique needs and life circumstances. Therefore, the perception of adult learners as completely self-governing in their educational journey may be a simplification that does not recognize the complex web of challenges they face. It may be imperative that educational institutions consider these multifaceted barriers when designing policies and support mechanisms for this diverse cohort of learners.

Turning our attention to institutional aspects, one finds that the educational landscape itself could be partly responsible for the impediments that adult learners face. Although colleges and universities are becoming increasingly diverse, many people still adhere to a pedagogical framework primarily designed for the 18 to 23-year-old age group. This mismatch can lead to an incongruent learning environment in which adult learners can feel out of place or even marginalized.

The conventional academic calendar, with its rigid semester-based structure, poses additional challenges to adult learners. Such inflexibility is often incompatible with the unpredictable schedules that most adult learners must face, predominantly because of work or family commitments. It should be noted that this inflexibility can create a psychological barrier to entry for potential adult students, considering a return to formal education.

To truly level the playing field for adult learners, a change in basic assumptions may be necessary within educational institutions. This would involve adopting flexible course schedules and alternative delivery methods. They also involve rethinking assessment strategies and pedagogical approaches. By embracing a more inclusive model of education that respects and accommodates the diverse needs of all learners, institutions could make the challenging landscape of adult education less daunting. That way, they may open avenues for genuine lifelong learning.

-6-

ADULTS IN COLLEGES AND UNIVERSITIES

The prevalent perception portrays college students as young individuals. They navigate the labyrinthine hallways of dormitories. All this while enjoying their first taste of unsupervised life. This notion, to a considerable extent, consists of half-truths and simplifications. Although it captures the experience of a segment of the student population, it inadvertently omits the diverse range of learners that populate higher education institutions.

A university campus often serves as a proverbial playground for students. It offers them a space to explore their newfound autonomy. With their eyes away from the watchful eyes of parents or legal guardians, many students relish the opportunity to express themselves freely. This setting enables them to challenge conventions, question societal norms, and, indeed, experiment with varying aspects of adult life. This notion of a carefree, experimental college life has become so entrenched that it often overshadows the lived experiences of a sizable portion of the student body.

Not all experiences of freedom manifest themselves as reckless abandon or youthful folly. Consider a young adult whose education occurred under rigorous parental supervision. For such an individual, the college environment serves as an inaugural stage for the exercise of personal freedoms. On the contrary, for older adult learners who have already navigated the complexities of work and family responsibilities, college represents not a departure from, but a continuation of, their mature structured lives.

A mosaic of misconceptions colors our understanding of college life, some stemming from observed behaviors, while others are mere fabrications or idealized versions of adulthood. Unfortunately, some of these misconceptions gain so widespread acceptance that they influence educational policies and teaching strategies. Stereotypes about the "typical" college student, a case in point, an older person in school, become so embedded in an educational discourse that they can inadvertently shape the experiences of all students, regardless of their age, thus affecting the effectiveness of educational outcomes.

Faculty members, particularly those of an older generation, often have a condescending or even paternalistic perspective toward their students. This viewpoint manifests itself not only in the academic domain but extends into the realm of personal development and social comportment. Professors, driven by this mindset, may find it incumbent on them to inculcate students with good manners and social etiquette. Although the imparting of these values often occurs through subtle cues or indirect communication, the underlying assumption remains clear: educators perceive a certain lack of maturity or social skill among their students that they believe necessitate correction.

This approach to teaching, which incorporates elements of moral and social guidance, can become problematic. It potentially undermines the agency of adult learners, young and old, who enter educational settings with a myriad of life experiences and wisdom. This attitude, unintentionally or otherwise, can serve to infantilize these learners, reducing their educational journey to a prescribed path defined by the educator's personal beliefs and values.

This mindset further raises questions about the boundary between academic instruction and personal development within an educational context. It prompts educators to grapple with the extent of their roles. Are they merely disseminators of academic knowledge, or should they also serve as architects of character and social acumen? Although the answer remains debatable, the paternalistic position risks imposing a singular, [possibly] outdated perspective on a diverse student body, thereby inhibiting the rich exchange of ideas and experiences that should characterize higher education.

ADULT SUPERVISION IN SCHOOLS

Certain school staff and faculty members sometimes harbor malicious intentions toward students they consider insolent or disruptive. The avenue for their punitive measures remains primarily academic in nature. It serves as a cautionary tale. This is about the hidden perils of higher education for adult learners.

Some professors have been known to give lower grades to students who submit assignments after the designated deadline, regardless of the quality or effort expended on the work. Such practices wield grading as a weapon. This puts students in a precarious position. They have limited avenues of redress. This phenomenon marks a tragic facet of higher education, where academic evaluations are transformed into punitive instruments, thus diminishing the educational experience of adult learners.

In a more subtle form of academic coercion, other faculty members employ astuteness in structuring their courses. Through a labyrinthine array of assignments, including but not limited to readings and online postings, these professors virtually eliminate any prospect of leisure time for their students. Students are anchored at library desks, entangled in an endless cycle of academic labor.

Many professors, especially those teaching compulsory courses, perceive this heavy workload as a form of necessary supervision. They treat their students as if they were children in need of constant supervision. This approach raises ethical questions about the agency and autonomy of adult learners, many of whom bring a wealth of life experience to the classroom and have chosen to pursue higher education voluntarily.

Students seldom have viable options to challenge these paternalistic practices. Such an approach might be justifiable when dealing with young children. But this way of doing things, or this modus operandi, becomes increasingly problematic when applied to adult learners who do not require external supervision to commit to their academic endeavors.

Issues such as the ones listed earlier do not necessarily discriminate based on age. Older people who pursue higher education face the same pitfalls and frustrations, which younger learners experience, though there are noteworthy exceptions. Adult learners can begin to feel unappreciated and marginalized, which can further exacerbate the divide between them and the educational institutions that should, in theory, facilitate their intellectual growth and personal development.

The harsh reality of such an educational system can wreck the psyche and ambitions of the learner. This setting can intensify the compulsion to withdraw from a course. It fosters a corrosive environment. This milieu can ignite conflicts not only with professors, but also with fellow students. In some extreme cases, disillusioned students may sever all links with their educational ambitions. They view them as unattainable under the prevailing conditions.

The Council for Adult and Experimental Learning (CAEL) has shed light on another dimension of this challenge. Their research indicated that numerous higher education institutions remain inadequately equipped to meet the unique needs of adult learners (CAEL, 2000). In this context, older learners often find themselves isolated. They struggle to navigate an environment designed primarily for young adults.

Incongruities between older learners and traditional educational settings often extend beyond mere academic complications; they may take the form of pedagogy and personal issues. Although the younger demographic may find current educational structures suitable, older adults often face challenges arising from conflicting responsibilities at home or in the workplace.

These stressors compound the difficulties they already face in the academic setting. They exacerbate their struggles. They also leave them stranded in an inhospitable environment. Therefore, adult learners face a series of multifaceted obstacles that question the inclusivity and adaptability of current higher education systems.

A RUDE AWAKENING

The propensity for adult learners to disengage from their educational journey stems not merely from personal whims, but often from the prevailing culture within the educational institutions themselves. Contrary to widely held belief, adult learners often find themselves navigating an educational process over which they exert minimal control. The inability to steer one's educational path often originates from the rigidity of the system, where academic culture can suppress enthusiasm and hinder learning.

In my own academic past, I encountered a professor known for her challenging demeanor. Initially, I dismissed the derogatory nicknames and disparaging comments about the professor that I had heard from fellow students. I considered them exaggerated folklore. "No one is actually that way," I thought to myself. Most of her courses were prerequisites for my field. This left me with little choice. I had to enroll and judge for myself the validity of these claims.

Enrolling in a required course offered by the professor in 2010 proved to be an eye-opening experience for me. From the outset, the professor wielded a palpable aura of intimidation. Her teaching style exhibited a condescending tone, while her syllabus read as a set of draconian laws aimed at elevating her own ego. Her classroom demeanor was reminiscent of a drill sergeant, more than an academic facilitator.

Soon, I discovered the unsettling truth behind the rumors. The professor consistently maintained a brusque disposition. Her lectures often spanned the entire class period. This eclipsed opportunities for fruitful discussions or queries.

The classroom environment morphed into something akin to an intellectual boot camp, where the primary lesson learned was not the course material but a profound sense of apprehension towards the professor herself. This experience illuminated the academic barriers adult learners can face; barriers built not by the complexity of the curriculum, but by the individuals entrusted with enriching our intellectual lives.

It became clear that the professor lacked even a basic modicum of human decency. She would berate the students for tardiness and ridicule them for asking questions that she deemed inappropriate. His continued defensive posture raised questions about her true motivation for being in academia. It appeared as if her classroom served as an outlet for her own personal frustrations, rather than a space dedicated to learning and intellectual growth.

Inhabiting such a fear-fueled learning environment was like undergoing a form of academic penance. The sadistic tendencies of the professor became increasingly clear; respect for the students was conspicuously absent from her teaching philosophy. As the semester progressed, I felt my enthusiasm for the course wane dramatically. Subsequent conversations with classmates revealed that I was not alone in my feelings.

Collective anxiety created a toxic atmosphere that eroded not only the quality of the educational experience but also our intrinsic motivation to learn. This type of pedagogical toxicity can derail the educational aspirations of adult learners. It instills in them a disenchantment. This disenchantment extends far beyond the walls of a single classroom. This unfortunate episode served as a glaring example of the academic hurdles adult learners can face, which often have less to do with the material and more to do with the individuals entrusted with delivering it.

AN ASYMMETRICAL RELATIONSHIP

In the 2011 academic year, I was enrolled in a course with a professor who had gotten widespread disdain on campus. The troubling element was the invincibility that enveloped this faculty member. She was not just tenured; she had amassed a litany of accolades and had wielded considerable influence in administrative roles within her department.

During a rare moment of class discussion, the professor dropped a revelation that left me astounded. She declared that the relationship between a student and a professor was "asymmetric," indicating that the interaction was "unidirectional." When asked to elaborate, she coldly stated: Professors have no obligations with students.

Furthering her provocative position, she articulated: "If a student dares to challenge a professor, the student is destined for defeat." She attributed this imbalance to the extensive institutional power professors command, backed by their respective departments. In contrast, she argued, students possessed "no power worthy of recognition by a professor or a department."

Such declarations sent waves of shock through me. The pieces of this strange puzzle came together. With a heavy heart, just a few weeks into the semester, I considered withdrawing from the course. I realized that the professor's conduct transcended mere rudeness; it veered into the realm of outright hostility. Her conduct implied that her faculty status granted her an unquestionable right to demean and belittle students. She was stripping them of their intrinsic value as human beings. She also disregarded their worth as learners.

After the sudden admission of the professor, I was completely disconnected from the educational content of the course. Her demeanor, which was unapologetically condescending, robbed me of my ability to concentrate in the class. I averted her gaze. I was afraid to close my eyes to someone who so brazenly diminished her students.

Although I completed the course, my grade reflected my internal struggle rather than my academic potential. My grade became an inconsequential concern; my main objective turned out to be to survive what had become a painful educational ordeal. Each day intensified my excitement at the end of the semester. This marked one of the most distressing periods of my academic life.

During that tumultuous academic year, my mind was a battlefield of conflicting thoughts. I wrestled with the tension between acknowledging the professor's prerogative to dictate course structure and discipline and my inherent belief that the educational relationship should not be one-sided. I had basic rights, and the professor had an obligation to respect those rights. However, as the weeks unfolded, it became abundantly clear that she had no duty to treat me, or any student, with a modicum of dignity. I felt relegated to the status of a mere child within her educational domain.

In response to her aloof and domineering attitude, I walked on eggshells, cautiously avoiding any behavior that might draw her ire. Fear of verbal reprimand paralyzed my participation in class discussions. I hesitated to voice any opinion, lest I utter something that could serve as fodder for her public criticism. In an environment where learning should have been the paramount objective, I can honestly say that I did not acquire meaningful knowledge from that course.

The notion that the professor wielded unchecked power within the classroom became an insurmountable obstacle to my academic engagement. It fueled a debilitating fear that she could act with impunity, free to mistreat her students without repercussions. This perception exerted a negative influence on my willingness to learn. It undermined my educational experience in the course.

The realization that the academic setting could become a space devoid of accountability or empathy was both disheartening and demotivating. It led me to question the very essence of what a learning environment should represent. This understanding affected not just my performance in that course but also my broader perspective on the educational system.

In the aftermath of such an unsettling experience, I understood the power dynamics at the university. The professor's notion of "asymmetry" between students and faculty made me reflect on systemic issues far beyond a single classroom. Could an institution designed to educate also have built-in mechanisms that push faculty to marginalize their students?

One could argue that the tenure status and institutional influence of a professor, as in the case of my professor, could create an environment that suppresses not only dissent but also the collaborative spirit that should be at the heart of education. This experience also piqued my interest in examining the effectiveness channels for student grievances, many of which I found to be not as effective. If a professor could act with such impunity, it suggested the absence of robust safeguards to keep educators accountable for their actions and teaching methods. It left me wondering: How many other students had their academic journeys tarnished by educators who forgot that their role is not just to instruct, but also to inspire?

Beyond the academic realm, this ordeal had lingered psychological impacts. The suppression of student voices and the stifling of academic curiosity led to a sort of cognitive dissonance, a conflict between my idealized vision of higher education as a platform for intellectual growth and the stark reality of encountering a professor who embodied the antithesis of this vision. To reckon with this dissonance was not just a philosophical exercise, but also an emotional labor that called into question the purpose and the promise of higher education itself.

A Social Stream

-7-

A CULTURE OF ACADEMIC CONTEMPT

Confronted by a hostile professor as a graduate student, my experience was not an anomaly. Numerous college students, especially adult learners, navigate the treacherous waters of unfavorable pedagogical interactions. For mature students, these encounters have the potential for severe consequences. They range from psychological distress to academic failure.

Before this unsettling academic journey, I viewed myself as a diligent student. Availability, active participation in class discussions, and timely submission of assignments characterized my approach to learning. This disheartening encounter with a disgruntled professor cast a shadow over my entire educational outlook.

Feeling trapped rather than intellectually stimulated, I wrestled with existential questions about my role in the educational landscape. The classroom became an environment laden with fear, a place I wanted to escape rather than a sanctum for intellectual engagement. The days when education seemed a fulfilling endeavor; it metamorphosed into an oppressive obligation that I was eager to abandon.

Unfortunately, my academic performance fell considerably. Despite my investment in the course, I earned a disappointing grade that undeniably left me distraught. Given the intimidating demeanor of the professor, it was difficult to confront her. She had a penchant for disregarding student input. Therefore, challenging her appeared to be an insurmountable obstacle. This isolated course significantly reduced my overall grade point average (GPA). It added to an already harrowing experience.

How could this have happened to me? I was an adult learner. According to popular belief, adult learners are in charge of their learning experience. But this was not the case for me in the mentioned course.

What became increasingly clear to me was not just the personal impact. There was also a larger and disturbing trend within the American educational system. There was a widespread culture of insensitivity toward adult learners. Those assigned with the responsibility of facilitating a seamless transition for adults reentering academia were woefully indifferent to the unique challenges we face. Instead of elevating individuals through education, the existing infrastructure appeared to be geared towards undermining one's self-esteem and diminishing one's essence as a student.

A climate of academic disdain has the power to severely affect the learner, particularly those in adult education. In such an environment, a mature student might find their enthusiasm waning, not solely for the specific subject matter, but potentially for the broader educational experience. Unlike traditional younger students, adult learners often perceive education as a multidirectional enterprise. They seek not only to absorb knowledge, but also to contribute to the academic discourse.

Contrary to stereotypical beliefs, adult learners generally do not have egocentric tendencies. Rarely do they aim to command the spotlight in the educational arena. However, they anticipate a modicum of respect and, in certain contexts, a level of parity with their instructors. Such expectations, sadly, often set the stage for potential conflict within the classroom. This results in a strained instructor-student dynamic.

The problem intensifies when one considers the unique assets that adult learners bring to the academic table. Many have extensive professional backgrounds. They also have a wealth of real-world experience. This is supposed to enrich the classroom dialogue. These learners often feel the obligation to impart their specialized knowledge to their peers. However, this well-intended act of sharing may not always be well with faculty members. Some professors could perceive this sharing as an intrusion into their pedagogical domain. This could trigger sentiments of insecurity. It could also lead to intellectual intimidation.

CLASSROOM MANAGEMENT ISSUES

In the landscape of adult education, I observed a peculiar phenomenon in which instructors seemed to engage in a contest of wit and attention with their students. Some professors appeared to be happy to maintain a centralized focus. They enjoyed their role as epicenters of classroom activity. Challenging the established hierarchy meant risking punishment by the professor.

Tension would arise when adult students, particularly the most curious ones, unknowingly disrupted the professor's air of intellectual invincibility. This reality not only produced palpable discomfort within the classroom, but also created a rift between instructors and students. Over time, my original observation, influenced by a particular antagonistic professor who insisted that professors owe no responsibilities to students, appeared less like an isolated stance and more like an institutional ethos.

Throughout my American educational journey, the repetitive chorus of similar experiences from various corners solidified my understanding of a pervasive culture among faculty. This culture systematically mocks students, often invoking minor disagreements or inconsequential factors as justification. I discerned a recurring motif in the American academic setting. Here, the odds favored the professor in any form of contention with students, especially during the culminating stages of a course.

Success in this scenario appeared to be less about academic prowess and more about one's readiness to respond to the inherent power dynamics of the classroom. Although this act of self-effacement might be manageable for younger learners, it poses a substantial hurdle for adult students. It frequently culminates in strained relationships and, in many cases, an unsatisfactory educational experience.

ACADEMIC DESPOTISM

In the corridors of American higher education, there is a great degree of academic despotism. Professors have the ultimate authority to assess the scholastic value of a student, a power often misused to retaliate against those considered insubordinate or intellectually inferior. This authoritative grip perpetuates a hierarchy in which the student, ironically, the consumer of education, often finds himself at the receiving end of arbitrary judgments.

Far from being a uniquely American construct, the principle that students should remain powerless in their own educational journey bears the imprimatur of a time-honored pedagogical tradition. This paradigm has often relegated students to mere receptors in the educational process, subservient figures expected to receive (albeit gratefully) whatever wisdom a professor deigns to dispense. One could argue that this asymmetric professor-student relationship has long rendered students as subordinate entities within the academic arena.

In the eyes of educators, the classroom transforms into a quasi-feudal domain where they rule supreme. Here, the students must comply. They adopt a posture of servility. Their role is strictly defined by a professorial fiat. The student becomes an object, not a subject, a passive recipient, rather than an active participant in the pursuit of knowledge.

In such a setting, students must adhere to the unilateral academic criteria set forth by the professor, who retains exclusive rights to the informational goods on offer. Deviation from established norms subjected the student to punitive measures imposed at the discretion of the professor. This authoritarian ecosystem does not only hinder academic progress; it poses also poses significant psychological implications and fosters an educational totalitarianism that leaves no room for dissent.

The scenario becomes more complex and disconcerting in the context of adult education. Thomas (2005) explains the importance of academic institutions in comprehending and accommodating the unique requirements of adult learners. The author emphasizes the need for faculty and administrators to acknowledge the diverse fabric of age, gender, race, and social background that adult learners bring to the academic setting (Thomas, 2005). Although these prescriptions may seem straightforward, their actual implementation remains a labyrinthine challenge.

The enduring nature of the academic hierarchy, despite being a topic of discussion for more than a decade, suggests an unsettling stagnation in educational reform. Students, particularly those in higher education, are in an unenviable position of having to navigate this rigid system without assistance. Therefore, the call to treat adult learners with the respect they deserve is not only timely but also critically necessary.

In the landscape of American higher education, the maltreatment of adult learners remains a pressing issue. Even as academic dialogue proliferates, there seems to be an inertia that prevents any substantive change. This inertia results in a status quo that unfairly disadvantages adult learners. It reinforces a troubling pattern of injustice and neglect.

One must consider the incongruity between the robust discussions that have characterized this topic for years and the stark reality that tangible improvements are scarce. This points to deep-rooted institutional resistance that hampers progress. Despite the passing of time, the call for equitable treatment of adult learners in the American educational system remains an urgent demand that requires immediate redress.

THWARTING ACADEMIC GOALS

In higher education, the objectives of animating adult learners diverge markedly from those of traditional students. Although the latter may revel in the social ecosystems of academic campuses, adult learners show a noticeable absence from such spaces. Their commitments outside of educational settings: the rigors of work and family responsibilities often preclude them from lingering on school grounds between classes.

Regarding academic performance, adult learners often show an unmistakable focus. They aim unwaveringly for stellar outcomes, manifested in their relentless pursuit of high-grade point averages (GPA). The intention of these learners can be unequivocal. That is, they seek to achieve metrics that serve as unequivocal indicators of their academic prowess, which is also a feat that they believe should not be compromised for any reason, least of all capriciousness from instructors.

Adult learners show a pragmatism that extends to their career choices, a dimension of their lives often already carved out by practical considerations. Unlike their younger counterparts, who may still navigate the exploratory phase of their vocational lives, adult learners typically select educational paths that promise to maximize employment opportunities. Thus, their academic endeavors are meticulously tailored to match existing or aspirational roles in the professional world.

Adult learners often enter the classroom with substantial preexisting knowledge of their chosen fields. Far from being empty vessels waiting for the professor's wisdom, they view the educational experience to a specific end: the acquisition of an academic degree that improves employment or facilitates a life transition. Their focus remains sharply aligned with this endgame; they wish to invest time and effort only in what directly furthers their goals.

Adult learners operate with a greater sense of the value of time. They manifest a utilitarian attitude towards their educational journey. They desire to absorb only what will be of direct utility in their future endeavors. Extraneous courses or internships that do not align with their precise academic or career objectives do a little favor in their educational scheme.

The misalignment between the needs of adult learners and the rigidity of academic institutions extends beyond the simple dynamics of the classroom. Consider the inflexibility of curricular structures that do not pay attention to the multifaceted lives of mature students. These individuals often juggle work commitments, family responsibilities, and at times, even previous educational or vocational experiences that could enrich the academic environment. Conventional academic systems rarely offer the latitude for these learners to capitalize on their life experience for academic credit or shape their educational trajectory in a way that reflects their diverse needs.

Financial considerations also present a unique set of challenges for the adult learner. Unlike traditional students who may rely on family support or scholarships targeted at younger demographics, adult learners often self-finance their education. The pressure to return on investment is palpable and immediate. They require educational outcomes that translate directly into career advancement or job security. However, existing financial aid structures rarely address these nuanced needs.

Discrimination, subtle but discernible, poses another significant obstacle. This takes form not only in terms of age but also encompasses the intersectionality of age with gender, race, and socioeconomic status. The collective impact of these factors can significantly reduce the quality of education experience for the adult learner.

The systemic challenges facing adult learners in higher education are diverse and complex. The absence of supportive measures and a pedagogical framework that understands and accommodates the unique circumstances of older learners signifies a glaring oversight in contemporary education. A reevaluation of institutional strategies and policies aimed at inclusivity and respect for diverse learning needs emerges as an imperative for educational reform.

-8-

ASSESSMENT OF ENVIRONMENTAL ISSUES

In higher education, adult learners navigate a labyrinth of challenges that extend beyond the classroom. They face financial constraints, social predicaments, and psychological trials, often carrying the burden of these multifaceted issues without institutional support. To add another layer of complexity, these challenges often intersect with environmental factors. They magnify their impact on academic success. They also affect personal well-being.

The literature reveals that adult learners often carry family responsibilities. This places them in a dichotomy of roles. They are stretched thinly across the personal and educational domains. McGroarty (1993) illustrated that these learners often serve as the foundation of their households. They care for the needs of the dependents. They do this before their own educational pursuits (McGroarty, 1993). Their quest for higher learning often takes a backseat, suffers from neglect, or faces an indefinite postponement.

The transition from a professional setting to an academic setting presents a unique set of challenges. This contributes to a high attrition rate among adult learners. Institutions often overlook the urgent need for resources to help mature students manage life's complexities while striving for educational advancement. Therefore, their rate of success in achieving their educational goals can remain disappointingly low.

The disparities between traditional and non-traditional student outcomes garnered scholarly attention as early as the turn of the century. Osgood-

Treston (2001) highlighted a longitudinal study, which revealed a disconcerting trend. That is, traditional students exhibited a noticeably higher graduation rate compared to their nontraditional counterparts, who are adult learners (Osgood-Treston, 2001). The findings underscored the additional responsibilities that mature students should assume, responsibilities that often compromise their educational endeavors. This observation continues to be relevant. It affirms the systemic challenges that still plague adult learners. These challenges are prevalent in today's academic landscape.

Examining the issue through a social lens reveals that adult learners frequently find themselves in a state of discordance with the prevailing social environments within educational institutions. This sense of discord intensifies when examined from a cultural perspective. It reveals that such environments often clash with the values. Practices or lifestyles that adult learners hold dear are often in conflict. Cultural incompatibilities not only form barriers to social integration but also pose significant challenges to academic assimilation.

The archetype of an adult learner often corresponds to individuals burdened with a variety of responsibilities that extend well beyond academic commitments. McGroarty (1993) noted that a substantial number of these learners are single parents juggling family obligations, and they commonly maintain full-time employment. For these individuals, the pursuit of higher education constitutes merely one component of an exhaustive list of daily responsibilities. Attending lectures or participating in academic activities does not mark the pinnacle of your daily routine but rather serves as another task in a long litany of obligations.

Given this intricate interplay of roles and responsibilities, adult learners find themselves at a unique intersection where the lines between work, family, and education blur. It becomes an exercise in balance, a constant reevaluation of priorities, and a test of resilience. Each role they occupy demands attention. This leaves little room for compromise or negotiation. Therefore, it presents challenges not only in academic realms but also in social and cultural spheres within the higher education setting.

SINGLE PARENTHOOD AND WORK

My childhood gave me a first-hand view of the hardships faced by adult learners, a perspective that came from watching my mother struggle to balance her family, professional and academic responsibilities. She openly admitted the daunting challenges that accompanied the Herculean task of fulfilling these divergent roles. Her confessions not only highlighted the grit required for adult learners, but also underscored the intricacies of their life paths.

Far from being an isolated example, my mother's academic journey is consistent with the experience of countless adult learners who navigate the turbulent waters of higher education today. An air of consensus prevails in stating the undeniable difficulty of being an adult learner. External factors proliferate. They may serve to deter or dissuade these individuals. These individuals may not continue their educational efforts. The allure of abandoning their academic pursuits is a temptation to which many succumb, thus truncating their educational journeys prematurely.

It is critical to note that the complexities faced by adult learners exhibit stark differences compared to their younger counterparts. College students, regardless of their age, find themselves routinely ensnared in a precarious balancing act between academic commitments and other life responsibilities. Pressure often pushes them to the brink. At this juncture, abandoning educational pursuits becomes not only a viable option. It also becomes an attractive option.

Adding another layer to this intricate scenario is the often-overlooked reality that a considerable proportion of college students are simultaneously engaged in employment. White (2015) illuminated this trend by referencing a study conducted by Georgetown University. The study revealed that in the last two decades, an astonishing 70% of college students have found it necessary to work while pursuing their studies (White, 2015). This empirical evidence further highlights the multidimensional challenges young and old learners must face to achieve academic success.[1]

The findings of a seminal study by Carnevale, Smith, Melton, and Price (2015) shed light on the complex relationship between employment and higher education. An astonishing 14 million college students found it difficult to harmonize their academic and professional commitments (Carnevale et al., 2015). The study further illuminates that such challenges are not limited by

---

[1] Please see the full report here. https://1gyhoq479ufd3yna29x7ubjn-wpengine.netdna-ssl.com/wp-content/uploads/Working-Learners-Report.pdf

age or academic level, but are widespread in both traditional and adult learners (Carnevale et al., 2015).

Of note is the demographic composition of this working-student population. The study highlights that one-third of these working learners are aged 30 years or older (Carnevale et al., 2015). Quite a few of them have parental responsibilities. The report offers convincing statistics. It shows that 25% of adult learners balance full-time employment (Carnevale et al., 2015). They are also actively participating in an educational program. These statistics take an even more astonishing turn when considering that 40% of undergraduate students and a whopping 76% of graduate students work no less than 30 hours per week (Carnevale et al., 2015).

Although the numbers may be confusing, they do not encapsulate only the lived experiences of adult learners. As White (2015) astutely observes, the trend of students combining work with education has been on the rise since the 1970s. This long-standing trend suggests a continually evolving landscape in which students, regardless of their age, are increasingly engaged in employment while pursuing higher education. It raises critical questions about the support structures needed to facilitate this dual engagement and optimize the outcomes for all the students involved.

In a study conducted by Osgood-Treston (2001), it was found that attrition rates among older adults in educational institutions were exceptionally high, with external responsibilities and lack of program satisfaction being significantly contributing factors. In particular, these dropouts are not merely sporadic occurrences. Instead, they reflect a trend, which is also rising at an alarming rate. The implications of such a trend extend far beyond individual disappointments; they underscore systemic failures to adequately accommodate the needs of this growing segment of the student body.

Park and Choi (2009) extended this dialogue. They highlighted the migration of adult learners from traditional college settings to online platforms (Park & Choi, 2009). Although this transition may initially seem like a step toward resolving the compatibility issue between older students and traditional educational formats, it introduces a new set of challenges. Online education, despite its flexibility and convenience, does not universally serve as an effective substitute for the adult learner (Park & Choi, 2009). The absence of interpersonal interaction, as well as other factors inherent in online learning environments, can exacerbate rather than improve the academic difficulties faced by this demographic (Park & Choi, 2009).

The research illustrated above presents a fascinating but concerning panorama of adult education. It depicts an educational landscape that seems increasingly inhospitable to adult learners. This pushes them toward alternatives. These options may not adequately address your unique needs or aspirations. These findings call higher education stakeholders to reconsider current models and critically think about inclusivity and effectiveness for a student body that defies traditional age norms.

Online Alternative

In recent years, the landscape of online education has undergone a transformative shift. It elevates the rigor and expectations of courses. Once perceived as an easier route to an education, these platforms now deliver courses that not only challenge but also demand a high level of academic engagement. This transformation calls into question the efficacy of online programs in serving the unique needs of adult learners, who often juggle multiple responsibilities.

Adult learners face severe limitations in their time and energy. This inhibits their full participation in online educational settings. Online forums, integral to the modern online educational experience, rarely witness active participation from this demographic. Assignments are a burden rather than an educational experience, and the conspicuous absence of academic support mechanisms further disempowers these students. Therefore, the online educational sphere may not be the ideal path for adults looking for a formal academic degree.

The quantitative survey by Park and Choi (2009) revealed an intricate web of factors that cause adult learners to sever their educational pursuits. From family to organizational support, from motivational dimensions such as satisfaction and relevance to individual attributes such as age and gender, each aspect plays a role in these educational outcomes. Concurrently, the adult learner does not shed other roles when assuming the student's identity; rather, the pressures of parenting, employment, and partnerships continue to exert their force. Over time, these cumulative responsibilities can become a daunting burden, too heavy to bear along with academic commitments. This amalgam of roles and responsibilities requires a re-evaluation of how educational systems can adapt to serve this multifaceted student body effectively.

Single parenthood emerges as a dominant factor that leads adult learners to leave educational pathways prematurely. Navigating the labyrinthine challenges exclusive to single parenthood, ranging from childcare to financial stressors, amplifies levels of anxiety and emotional turbulence. Faced with such an overwhelming array of stressors, most adult learners not only suspend their educational pursuits, but also abandon their career aspirations completely.

Dealing with these issues is rarely transient for adult learners; they extend throughout their academic tenure. Therefore, the conundrum becomes not merely one of initial entry into higher education, but of sustained engagement and eventual success. Developing a robust skill set that would allow for triumph in the academic arena while simultaneously managing single parenthood is a formidable challenge that often eludes most adult learners.

This grim reality calls for a thoughtful examination of how academic institutions and support networks can intervene to ease the disproportionate burdens imposed by this demographic. The aim should be to facilitate not only their survival, but also their thriving in higher educational settings, which must be against the backdrop of their multifaceted lives.

The nuances of individual circumstances cannot be overstated. Although the challenges associated with single-headed households stand out, confrontations with capricious staff or faculty serve as additional barriers that only exacerbate the plight of adult learners. Navigating these intricate dynamics without support often results in disappointment, if not outright disenchantment with the educational system.

This added layer of complexity raises questions about the readiness of academic institutions to meet the unique needs and challenges of adult learners. Schools equip their staff and faculty with the tools necessary to understand and help this demographic effectively? The answer, for a considerable number of cases, appears to be negative.

Adult learners, particularly those who reenter academia at a later stage in life, find themselves in a labyrinth of challenges that go beyond textbooks and classrooms. Systemic problems in educational settings combine with personal and family pressures to create a multifaceted and often discouraging experience. Accordingly, targeted interventions and educational reforms may be necessary to foster a more inclusive and supportive environment for this critical population.

School Culture and Adult Learners

In the United States, a substantial number of adult learners originate in foreign countries. They introduce a variety of cultural complexities into the academic landscape. Among these, English as a Second Language (ESL) students bring unique cultural perspectives that often diverge from those of their domestic counterparts. The heterogeneity of cultural backgrounds creates distinctive expectations about educational settings and interactions. This creates a crucible for potential misunderstandings.

When such individuals matriculate into American universities and colleges, they arrive armed with expectations shaped by their cultural background. This anticipation often conflicts with the comparatively lax pedagogical methods commonly used in American classrooms. The divergence can cause what many describe as a cultural shock. This can destabilize the learning experience of these adult learners.

McGroarty (1993) postulated that these culturally induced expectations extend far beyond mere personal preferences. They have the ability to drastically influence the perception of an adult learner of the educational setting, which can significantly inhibit their enthusiasm for participating in learning activities. McGroarty further illuminated that most adult learners expect instructors to maintain an authoritative demeanor in the classroom. Erosion of these conventional boundaries, such as an instructor referring to students by their first names or permitting the free movement of students during a lecture, can evoke profound dismay or even offense. Then, it becomes imperative to recognize and address these cultural intricacies to create an inclusive and effective learning environment.

Navigating the labyrinthine intricacies of adult education undeniably poses formidable challenges. Although numerous initiatives have been implemented to alleviate the struggles faced by this demographic, the inherent difficulties persist. Although commendable, efforts have not yet managed to transform the essential nature of the adult learning experience in America.

Far from a leisurely stroll through academic gardens, the journey of adult learning in the United States remains fraught with obstacles. This reality underscores the imperative for relevant systemic changes to facilitate the academic pursuits of nontraditional learners. It is essential to recognize that the complexities and pressures of educational attainment do not discriminate according to age. Success in the educational realm is rarely, if ever, the byproduct of mere coincidence or minimal exertion; it requires a concerted and ongoing commitment.

The issue of adult learning extends far beyond the institutional walls. It penetrates the very fabric of the society in which these learners exist. A kaleidoscope of factors, economic, psychological, and social, interact to shape the adult learning experience in a unique way. Older learners, to illustrate, often bring a wealth of real-world experience into the classroom. This reality could enrich the educational environment for all participants. However, these same learners often face unparalleled barriers in the form of family commitments, career responsibilities, and social expectations.

Although adult learners enrich the academic environment with their unique perspectives and experiences, they also face specific hurdles that younger, more traditional students may not face. These include issues such as ageism in the classroom, limited familiarity with new educational technologies, and outdated or rusty study skills. Financial burdens also often weigh heavily, especially for those who have families to support or mortgages to pay.

Such a complex web of variables requires a multifaceted approach to improving the adult education experience. Individual institutions, government agencies, and community organizations must engage in concerted efforts to remove barriers and create pathways to success. Only through an integrated strategy can the intricate challenges faced by adult learners in the United States be addressed effectively. Such a strategy would not only represent an investment in the learners themselves, but also an investment in the broader social and economic well-being of the nation.

FINAL WORDS

CONCLUSION

In his riveting state-of-the-union address in 2009, President Barack Obama issued a clarion call to parents across the nation. He urged them to increase their participation in their children's educational journeys and return to school themselves (C-SPAN, 2010; Obama, 2009). He made a compelling point: "A good education is no longer just a pathway to opportunity. It is a prerequisite" (Obama, 2009).

The President did not stop there. He extended his appeal to the broader American population, stating: "Every American must commit to at least one year or more of higher education or career training." This can be a community college or four-year school, vocational training, or an apprenticeship" (Obama, 2009). According to Obama, there was no room for ambivalence; every American needed more than a mere high school diploma to compete effectively in the global labor market (Obama, 2009).

Although most Americans may have taken Obama's impassioned words to heart, formidable obstacles remain on the path to higher education. This is especially true for adult learners, for whom the academic landscape often appears not only steep, but almost insurmountable. The existing educational system scarcely provides rapid pathways tailored to the unique challenges and needs of these mature individuals.

To further complicate matters, the concept of adult education remains hazy and diffused in policy discussions without a clear definition or direction. Adult learners are devoid of a unified voice in political and policy-making circles. The policies currently in force about adult education demonstrate little efficacy in resolving the specific issues facing adult learners. These individuals often find themselves in a precarious situation, caught between the demands of life and the constraints of a system that seems not to have been designed with them in mind.

Adult learners, despite their distinct characteristics compared to their younger counterparts, face a myriad of challenges that span political, social, emotional, and environmental dimensions. Higher education institutions must recognize the demands of adult learning. This reality requires a divergent approach and specialized resources dedicated to adult learning in general.

In a similar vein, there is a glaring deficit in the staffing departments of many colleges and universities, which often lacks the expertise needed to address the unique issues faced by adult learners. This shortfall becomes even more critical against the backdrop of spiraling tuition costs, a burden frequently shouldered by adult students without the cushion of parental support.

Financial instability emerges as another powerful obstacle, particularly during challenging economic conditions. The need to service an ever-growing mountain of debt, from federal loans to personal loans, further complicates the situation. Complementing these financial woes is the need for adult learners to maintain employment while pursuing their studies, a requirement that exacerbates the likelihood of academic attrition.

Family dynamics, whether in single or dual parents' households, add yet another layer of complexity to the adult learning experience. Additional challenges come from various sources: lack of internal or external support systems, cultural factors, and commitments related to the job can all act as barriers to successful academic participation.

The cumulative weight of these stressors takes a heavy emotional toll on adult learners, often inducing levels of stress and anxiety that are incompatible with effective learning. Despite its critical importance, adult education remains one of the most overlooked issues plaguing the American educational landscape. It is an unfortunate reality that I experienced. However, through this short compilation, I wanted to illuminate this overlooked facet of the American educational narrative.

For several adult learners, abandoning an educational path often emerges as a more viable option than remaining in institutions that exhibit minimal interest in their intellectual or emotional well-being. Others may find themselves enticed by the allure of prestigious institutions only to discover a disconcerting indifference to their educational aspirations. Such scenarios capture the larger tragedy that affects the landscape of adult education.

Despite these daunting realities, adult education in America has an inherent duality. It can be as rewarding as challenging. For those who muster the necessary resilience and tenacity to overcome the numerous barriers inherent in the educational experience, the eventual reward can be deeply satisfying. In contrast, if these hurdles prove to be insurmountable, the arduous quest for an academic credential may well prove unfruitful. This reinforces the notion. For some, adult education remains an unattainable goal. This often-insurmountable reality captures the quintessence of adult learning in the United States.

REFERENCES

Andersson, P., Köpsén, S., Larson, A., & Milana, M. (2013). Qualification paths of adult educators in Sweden and Denmark. *Studies in Continuing Education, 35*(1), 102–118.

Angeliki, G., & Loukas, M. (2021). The integration of experiential techniques in adult education and the factors influencing their adoption. *International Journal of Research -GRANTHAALAYAH, 9*(7), Article 7. https://doi.org/10.29121/granthaalayah.v9.i7.2021.4127

Boyadjieva, P., & Ilieva-Trichkova, P. (2017). Between inclusion and fairness: Social justice perspective to participation in adult education. *Adult Education Quarterly, 67*(2), 97–117.

Brown, O. (1955). Brown v. Board of education.

Brown v. Board of Education, 347 US 483 (Supreme Court 1954).

Brown v. Board of Education, 349 US 294 (Supreme Court 1955).

CAEL. (2000). *Serving Adult Learners in Higher Education: Principles of Effectiveness.* Council for Adult and Experiential Learning. http://www.cael.org/pdf/publication_pdf/summary%20of%20alfi%20principles%20of%20effectiveness.pdf

Carnevale, A. P., Smith, N., Melton, M., & Price, E. W. (2015, October 28). Learning While Earning: The New Normal. *CEW Georgetown.* https://cew.georgetown.edu/cew-reports/workinglearners/

Cornell Law. (2010a, August 19). *Brown v. Board of Education (1954).* LII / Legal Information Institute. https://www.law.cornell.edu/supremecourt/text/347/483

Cornell Law. (2010b, August 19). *Plessy v. Ferguson (1896)*. LII / Legal Information Institute. https://www.law.cornell.edu/wex/plessy_v._ferguson_1896

C-SPAN (Director). (2010, January 27). *Pres. Obama's First State of the Union Address*. https://www.youtube.com/watch?v=6kYW_fgaDDM

Green, J. (1998). Andragogy: Teaching Adults. *Encyclopedia of Educational Technology, 11*, 2006.

Griffin v. School Bd. Of Prince Edward Cty., 377 US 218 (Supreme Court 1964).

History.com Editors. (2009, October 29). *Plessy v. Ferguson*. HISTORY. https://www.history.com/topics/black-history/plessy-v-ferguson

Huang, H. (2002). Toward constructivism for adult learners in online learning environments. *British Journal of Educational Technology, 33*(1), 27–37.

Jameson, M. M., & Fusco, B. R. (2014). Math anxiety, math self-concept, and math self-efficacy in adult learners compared to traditional undergraduate students. *Adult Education Quarterly, 64*(4), 306–322.

Jang, C. S., Lim, D. H., You, J., & Cho, S. (2021). Brain-based learning research for adult education and human resource development. *European Journal of Training and Development, 46*(5/6), 627–651. https://doi.org/10.1108/EJTD-02-2021-0029

Kara, M., Erdoğdu, F., Kokoç, M., & Cagiltay, K. (2019). Challenges faced by adult learners in online distance education: A literature review. *Open Praxis, 11*(1), Article 1. https://doi.org/10.5944/openpraxis.11.1.929

Kasworm, C. E. (2008). Emotional challenges of adult learners in higher education. *New Directions for Adult and Continuing Education, 120*, 27–34.

Knowles, M. S. (1980a). The modern practice of adult education: From pedagogy to andragogy. New York: Cambridge. *The Adult Education Company, 43*.

Knowles, M. S. (1980b). The modern practice of adult education (revised and updated).

Levenson, E., & Stapleton, A. (2018, May 10). *Yale officers admonished the white student who called police on a napping black student*. CNN.

https://www.cnn.com/2018/05/10/us/yale-student-nap-black-police-trnd/index.html

Linder, D. (2019). *Separate but Equal: Segregation in the Public Schools*. Exploring Constitutional Law. http://law2.umkc.edu/faculty/projects/ftrials/conlaw/sepbutequal.htm

Lockhart, P. R. (2018, November 14). *A professor called police on a black student for putting her feet up in class*. Vox. https://www.vox.com/identities/2018/11/14/18095516/university-texas-usta-black-student-professor-911-racism

Loveless, B. (2019). *Facing Your Fears of Returning to School as an Adult* [Blog]. Education Corner. https://www.educationcorner.com/fear-of-returning-to-school.html

Loveless, B. (2023). *Facing Your Fears of Returning to School as an Adult*. https://www.educationcorner.com/fear-of-returning-to-school.html

Mas' ud, B., & Imansari, N. (2022). The Role of Adult Education in Social Change: A Critical Review of Stephen Brookfield's Scholarship. *Jurnal Ilmiah Mandala Education, 8*(3).

McGroarty, M. (1993, July). *Cross-Cultural Issues in Adult ESL Classrooms*. Center for Adult English Language Acquisition. https://www.cal.org/caela/esl_resources/digests/cross_cultural.html

Milana, M., & McBain, L. (2014). Adult education in the United States of America: A critical examination of national policy (1998-2014). *Encyclopaideia, 18*(40). https://doi.org/10.6092/issn.1825-8670/4660

National Museum of American History, Behring Center. (n.d.). *Separate but Equal—Separate Is Not Equal*. Retrieved April 3, 2019, from https://americanhistory.si.edu/brown/history/1-segregated/separate-but-equal.html

Obama, B. (2009, February 24). President Obama's Address to Congress. *The New York Times*. https://www.nytimes.com/2009/02/24/us/politics/24obama-text.html

Osam, E. K., Bergman, M., & Cumberland, D. M. (2017). An integrative literature review on the barriers impacting adult learners' return to college. *Adult Learning, 28*(2), 54–60.

Osgood-Treston, B. (2001). Program Completion Barriers Faced by Adult Learners in Higher Education. *Academic Exchange Quarterly.* https://www.semanticscholar.org/paper/Program-Completion-Barriers-Faced-by-Adult-Learners-Osgood-Treston/4b23b0d30b7df3d5b6063b27954fec53834a623e

Park, J.-H., & Choi, H. J. (2009). Factors influencing adult learners' decision to drop out or persist in online learning. *Journal of Educational Technology & Society, 12*(4), 207–217.

Peterson, D. (2018, August 31). *Basic Information About Adult Education.* ThoughtCo. https://www.thoughtco.com/what-is-adult-education-31719

Plessy v. Ferguson, 163 US 537 (Supreme Court 1896).

Schneider, A., & Ingram, H. (1993). Social construction of target populations: Implications for politics and policy. *American Political Science Review, 87*(2), 334–347.

Separate but Equal: Segregation in the Public Schools. (n.d.). Retrieved June 3, 2016, from http://law2.umkc.edu/faculty/projects/ftrials/conlaw/sepbutequal.htm

Shen, Y. (2022). Application of Internet of Things in Online Teaching of Adult Education Based on Android Voice Assistant. *Mobile Information Systems, 2022.*

Sogunro, O. A. (2015). Motivating factors for adult learners in higher education. *International Journal of Higher Education, 4*(1), 22–37.

Thomas, E. (2005). The Adult Learner: Here to Stay. *Black Issues in Higher Education, 22*(6), 74.

Travers, N. (2013). Adult Education. In *Sociology of Education: An A-to-Z Guide* (Vol. 1, pp. 12–15).

Tzovla, E., & Kedraka, K. (2020). The Role of the Adults' Educator in Teacher Training Programs. *American Journal of Education and Learning, 5*(2), Article 2. https://doi.org/10.20448/804.5.2.152.158

UNESCO. (2017, May 2). *Adult education.* http://uis.unesco.org/en/glossary-term/adult-education

U.S. Department of Education. (2003). *Adult education and family literacy act, program year 2000-2001 report to Congress on state performance* [Offices; Indexes]. Adult Education, Office of Vocational and Adult Education. http://www.ed.gov/about/offices/list/ovae/index.html

U.S. Department of Education. (2005a). *Adult education* [Offices; Indexes]. US Department of Education (ED). http://www.ed.gov/about/offices/list/ovae/index.html

U.S. Department of Education. (2005b, December 19). *The Facts About...State Standards* [FAQs]. http://www2.ed.gov/nclb/accountability/standards/standards.html?src=az

U.S. Department of Education. (2013, September 17). *Adult Education and Family Literacy Act of 1998* [Laws]. https://www2.ed.gov/policy/adulted/leg/legis.html

Varkiani, A. M. (2018, August 3). *Police called because a Black student was eating lunch in her university's common room.* https://thinkprogress.org/smith-college-employee-call-police-black-student-eating-lunch-oumou-kanoute-83f8edfb70f6/

Vaske, J. M. (2001). Critical thinking in adult education: An elusive quest for a definition of the field. ProQuest Dissertations Publishing.

White, G. B. (2015, October 28). *The Struggle of Work-School Balance.* The Atlantic. https://www.theatlantic.com/business/archive/2015/10/work-school-balance-college/412855/

Wilson, J. P. (2012). The adult learner: The definitive classic in adult education and human resource development. *Industrial and Commercial Training, 44*(7), 438–439.

RECOMMENDED READINGS

Levenson, E., & Stapleton, A. (2018, May 10). Yale officers admonished the white student who called police on a napping Black student. Retrieved April 1, 2019, from CNN website: https://www.cnn.com/2018/05/10/us/yale-student-nap-black-police-trnd/index.html

Lockhart, P. R. (2018, November 14). A professor called police on a Black student for putting her feet up in class. Retrieved April 1, 2019, from Vox website: https://www.vox.com/identities/2018/11/14/18095516/university -texas-usta-black-student-professor-911-racism

Varkiani, A. M. (2018, August 3). Police called because a Black student was eating lunch in her university's common room. Retrieved April 1, 2019, from https://thinkprogress.org/smith-college-employee-call-police-black-student-eating-lunch-oumou-kanoute-83f8edfb70f6/

INDEX

The book includes a detailed index. Below are some of the words and phrases that had been echoed throughout the document. They are listed in alphabetic order, including cross-references and other pertinent listings.

A

ABOUT THE AUTHOR

Ben Wood Johnson is a social observer. He is a philosopher. He is also a multidisciplinary scholar. Dr. Johnson writes about law, legal theory, education, public policy, politics, race and crime, and ethics.

Dr. Johnson holds a Doctorate degree in educational leadership and master's degrees in political science, public administration, and criminal justice. He holds a bachelor's degree in criminal justice.

Dr. Johnson worked in law enforcement. He held position as anti-riot police officer, SWAT, diplomatic security, and counter ambush and terrorism. Dr. Johnson attended John Jay College of Criminal Justice.

Dr. Johnson speaks several languages, including French, Spanish, Portuguese, and Italian. He enjoys reading, poetry, painting, and music. You may contact Dr. Johnson using the information listed below.

Mailing Address

Tesko Publishing/Eduka Solutions
330 W. Main St #214
Middletown, PA 17057

Email

tkpubhouse@gmail.com

Also by Ben Wood Johnson

1. Racism: What is it?
2. Sartrean Ethics: A Defense of Jean-Paul Sartre as a Moral Philosopher
3. Jean-Paul Sartre and Morality: A Legacy Under Attack
4. Sartre Lives On
5. Forced Out of Vietnam: A Policy Analysis of the Fall of Saigon
6. Natural Law: Morality and Obedience
7. Cogito Ergo Philosophus
8. Le Racisme et le Socialisme: La Discrimination Raciale dans un Milieu Capitaliste
9. International Law: The Rise of Russia as a Global Threat
10. Citizen Obedience: The Nature of Legal Obligation
11. Jean-Jacques Rousseau: A Collection of Short Essays
12. Pennsylvania Inspired Leadership: A Roadmap for American Educators
13. Striving to Survive: The Human Migration Story
14. Postcolonial Africa Three Comparative Essays about the African State
15. Go Back Where You Came From

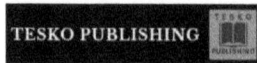

www.ingramcontent.com/pod-product-compliance
Lightning Source LLC
Chambersburg PA
CBHW030025290326
41934CB00005B/489